Mr & Mrs
WILKINSON'S
HOW IT IS AT HOME

**A COOKBOOK FOR
EVERY FAMILY**

Mr & Mrs
WILKINSON'S
HOW IT IS AT HOME

A COOKBOOK FOR
EVERY FAMILY

hardie grant books

Contents

THANK YOU

Thank you for taking the time to pick up this book, and as you read on we hope you find recipes to share with your loved ones as we do.

DEDICATION

To the ladies who raised us, Carol and Leah, and to our own two kids, Finn and Jay. We love you dearly and thank you for all the wonderful times we have had together.

So how is it really at home?

Well, let's start with what it's not. This book won't tell you how wonderful and perfect our lives are; how we get up every morning and bake bread, milk the cow and forage for nuts. It isn't all cheffy either and won't give you recipes that take hours to prepare and loads of different gadgets to make. And that's because we, the Wilkinson-Gibb clan, are like most of you, really busy getting on with a little thing called life. We are a simple, caring and loving family with a never-ending love for food, the seasons and Mother Nature and, hopefully, as you read through the chapters of this book you will get a sense of how we navigate our way through this crazy busy modern world – how we find the time to eat well and share stories and live our lives in our kitchen and house in the most stress-free way we can.

So who makes up our clan? Well, there's me (Mr), husband, father and son, Matt Wilkinson. Then there's wife, mother and daughter, Sharlee Gibb (Mrs) and our two pint-sized troublemakers – 'the hooligans', as we like to call them – Finn Thomas W-G and Jay Thomas W-G (yes, we were among those weirdos who hyphenated their children's surnames – I apologise now to 'FinnJay', it will get annoying writing your full names out, especially at the airport). Lastly, there's also a weird-looking-but-cute dog, Quincy, and two very vocal Sussex chooks, Major and Bryan.

I was brought up in Barnsley, South Yorkshire and left home at seventeen to head into the crazy world of hospitality, landing on the shores of Australia just before my twenty-first birthday. Sharlee was brought up in Eumundi, Queensland, and left home at eighteen, also to go into hospitality. Our paths nearly crossed in 2004, but for a week apart, when I had finished working at Vue de Monde after three years and Sharlee had just started. Let's just say, if we had met back then, this book would not have happened as I was this quiet, reserved lad from England and SG, well, let's just say that the word 'larrikin' describes it best!

While we've lived and breathed the industry for a long time (and both know nothing else, really). At home we like to cook simple dishes that are made from quality seasonal, ethically sourced ingredients as we believe the fundamentals of delicious food start with the produce you use. We hope you find the recipes on the pages that follow to be easy, tasty and fun and that you pick up a few tips on how to make your home cooking as stress-free as possible along the way.

EXPANDING YOUR REPERTOIRE

If we could achieve anything here we would love for you to gain 2–3 new dishes to add to your repertoire. I reckon at home most people have a repertoire of about 6–7 dishes that are their go-to dishes – these are the easy no-brainers. We're no different and, though we do try out new dishes and go back to things we haven't done for a while when we have time, when in doubt, when we don't have time to think about a new dish or when we simply can not be bothered, we fall back on our repertoire. My Mum's repertoire was classic English mother–style – thank god Jamie Oliver came along for British food at home is all I can say! Sunday was the classic roast with the best Yorkshire puddings and roast potatoes ever (Mum, just add a little more salt to your veggies please and maybe take the roast out 5 hours before you usually do). It was then a groundhog week of beef casserole, beef stroganoff (I loved this), spag bol', corned beef, shepherd's pie, cowboy dinner (see page 198) then back to the old Sunday roast. Leah, Sharlee's Mum, cooked wholesome food, so the kids ate a little differently to what most kids I reckon would have back then, her go-to dishes including spinach and feta pie, lentil spag bol', soy bean patties, lentil burgers, corned beef (at least we both had that in common), tuna mornay and lemon chicken. Imagine being one of Sharlee's friends at school and getting soy bean patties for dinner when you went around to play? It's amazing she had any friends at all!

TIPS

PREPARATION

If I can help you at all with cooking at home I can't tell you enough that it is all in the preparation. Making two meals when you have time, one for that moment and the other for the next day, can be a real saviour and is something we do a lot.

PLANNING

Planning your weekly food menu is a must. You might have gaps, but on a Sunday we write what we are thinking of eating, then we have a look at what we would need to buy, then we get it. Many people say 'I don't know what I want to eat now, let alone in a week'. That is rubbish. Just decide sooner and you'll be far less stressed when you have to cook quickly later.

AS A GUIDE

Please see our recipes as a guide, removing and adding ingredients to your liking. We eat seasonally, so if something isn't in season we change it to whatever is abundant and tasty.

TIME TO EAT

No matter where everybody is and what we are all up to, we always eat at 6 pm (when we were kid-less it was always 7.30 pm). If you don't have kids you may not want to do this every day of the week, but we find that it really works for us, putting structure into the day and reinforcing the importance of sitting down and eating together no matter what is going on.

THE TABLE

It's really important to enjoy your cooking but even more important is the act of sitting at the table together to eat it. The table brings us together, it's a place to share our stories, to laugh, to talk, and is somewhere for our children to learn life lessons and manners (like taking turns to speak). Most importantly, it's a place to share our love for each other and to remember that, as long as we are healthy, free and have a delicious meal in front of us, we are as wealthy as anyone.

DON'T STRESS

Finally, as a family we also like to go out to eat and we like to eat from the 'not-so-healthy' category too, loving fish 'n' chips, burgers and pizza just like, well, everybody. At home, there is also a small amount of processed food in our diet – we use those pre-made curry bases and satay sauces and are shockers for mainstream pre-sliced commercial bakery bread. Now, that doesn't mean I don't love sourdough but we make our choices and we think about them. If you're one of those people who feels guilty about your choices, don't be. Maybe look again at aspects of your diet but don't get yourself in a stress about it. I meet a lot of people who do and, well, life is too short.

What's in our spice drawer, cupboard, fridge & freezer ...

SPICE DRAWER*

Oregano

Fennel seeds

Nutmeg (whole and ground)

Dulse flakes

Red ginger powder

Ground turmeric

Cumin (whole and ground)

Coriander (whole and ground)

Cayenne pepper

Sweet smoked paprika

Garam masala

Ras el hanout

Kombu

Dried limes

Cardamom pods

Sumac

Dukkah

Yellow and black mustard seeds

Star anise

Cloves (whole and ground)

Cinnamon sticks

Kashmiri chilli powder

Bombay masala

* Where possible we use ethically sourced spices from a supplier called The Hidden Souk

CUPBOARD (BIODYNAMIC/ ORGANIC WHERE POSSIBLE)

Unbleached plain flour

Unbleached self-raising flour

Cornflour (cornstarch)

Semolina

Spelt flour

Baking powder

Bicarbonate of soda (baking soda)

Raw (demerara) sugar

Coconut sugar

Dried yeast

Rice (carnaroli, brown koshi, basmati, jasmine, wild)

Dried pasta shapes and spaghetti

Soba and udon noodles

Couscous

Red lentils

Rolled oats

Popcorn kernels

Cobram Estate olive oil (extra-virgin, lemon-infused and garlic-infused)

Vinegar (balsamic, apple cider, sherry and rice wine)

Soy sauce

White soy

Mirin

Sesame oil

Fish sauce

Ghee

Raw honey

Olsson's salt flakes

Kampot pepper (white and black)

Tinned tomatoes and passata (puréed tomatoes)

Tinned tuna in oil and water (a sustainably caught brand like Sirena)

Sugo (homemade, see page 160)

Tinned cannellini (lima) beans and chickpeas

Baked beans

Assorted jams and relishes

Mr Wilkinson's kasundi (see page 239) and pineapple chutney

Preserved lemons

Chia seeds

Maca powder

Raw cacao powder

Sesame seeds (black and white)

Pepitas (pumpkin seeds)

Raw almonds and cashews

Blonde sultanas (golden raisins)

Dried peaches, apricots and dates

Coconut flakes

Pine nuts

Brazil nuts

FRIDGE

Organic unsalted butter

Cheese (cheddar, parmesan, haloumi, Happy Cow)

Natural yoghurt (homemade, see page 26)

Demeter biodynamic milk

Organic almond milk

Wonton wrappers

Filo pastry

Free-range eggs (thanks, Bryan and Major)

Miso paste

Mustard (seeded, dijon)

Tomato paste (concentrated purée)

Mr Wilkinson's red sauce (see page 240)

Mr Wilkinson's brown sauce (see page 238)

Worcestershire sauce

Assorted chilli sauces (Chinese, Malaysian and Thai)

Strawberry jam

Pickles (always gherkins)

The Fermentary kimchi, raw kraut and red kraut

Stuff for stir-frys (kecap manis, black bean sauce and oyster sauce)

Maple syrup

Heilala vanilla paste

Promite

Hummus (homemade, see page 78)

Ginger

Capers

Good anchovies

Lemons

Kombucha

Cordial (homemade, see page 232)

Demeter biodynamic apple and pear juice

Beers, a bottle of sparkling wine, two white wines and a bottle of tonic water

FREEZER

Ice cream

Butter puff pastry

Bananas (peeled before freezing)

Peas

Parmesan rinds

Pesto

Stock (chicken and fish)

Australian prawns (shrimp), meat only

Meat (such as free-range turkey mince, Milawa free-range chicken thighs, Melbourne Pantry bacon and Warialda skirt steak) in portion-size packs

Last-minute dinners

We all know how busy life gets and that there are times when you're hungry and need something to cook quickly. The following dishes take between 20–40 minutes to prep, cook and wash up.

Recipes that make us smile

MATT'S FAVOURITES

CHOCOLATE & FENNEL COOKIES (PAGE 89)

BAKED VEGGIES & HALOUMI (PAGE 180)

BIBIMBAP (PAGE 148)

DIRTY MARTINI (PAGE 227)

DAD'S BURGERS (PAGE 200)

SHREDDED CHICKEN PASTA SOUP (PAGE 170)

SHARLEE'S FAVOURITES

BACON & EGG PIE (PAGE 134)

TURKEY NOT-SO-CHILLI (PAGE 150)

SCALLOPS WITH MISO BUTTER (PAGE 216)

PUMPKIN SCONES (PAGE 49)

ROAST CHICKEN (PAGE 140)

ZUCCHINI & FETA FRITTERS (PAGE 40)

THE HOOLIGANS' FAVOURITES

COWBOY DINNER (PAGE 198)

MUM'S RISOTTO (PAGE 172)

HAWAIIAN PIZZA (PAGE 60)

PRAWN DUMPLINGS WITH ASIAN GREENS (PAGE 158)

COTTAGE PIE (PAGE 131)

VAMPIRE PESTO PASTA (PAGE 202)

Breakfast

MR 'It'll set you up for the rest of the day, Matthew Thomas Wilkinson', was what I remember my Mum saying about breakfast as a kid. She didn't need to worry about me not eating it, though, I used to love it – always starting the day the same way with a glass of orange juice and a bowl of cereal (none of those cool ones you saw advertised on the TV, mind, just good old cornflakes or 'Weetabix', as they were known back in Yorkshire). That's now come full circle in my new family life and the boys are just the same, though they won't even stretch as far as cornflakes! Jay (hooligan number two) can eat up to six Weet-Bix at a go and even said to Sharlee one morning in the kitchen, 'Mumma, when I was a baby in your tummy and you were feeding me, did you give me Weet-Bix for breakfast?'

Personally, I love a good bacon and egg roll with brown sauce and have this often at Pope Joan when I get into work. It reminds me of Saturdays as a kid when Mum would give us one each with a bowl of Heinz tomato soup to dip it into as a treat. Being able to connect the past with the present through food memories like this is something that I love, and I'm conscious that Sharlee and I are creating similar experiences for our two boys for them to look back at with big smiles, or disgust, or love ... or all three.

Here we've included the recipes that make up our everyday breakfast staples, whether that be freshly squeezed juices or smoothies, simple pancakes or a warming bowl (or two) of porridge. There's nothing fancy here – owning a café where breakfast accounts for 40 per cent of the menu means we are often trying lots of exciting new options when out and about – but rather a selection of what we come back to time and time again. It's what we cook at home.

Smoothie

SERVES 1

MRS This is a great way to up your vegetable and nut quota for the day and is my go-to breakfast for school mornings. I use whatever's in the garden – kale, spinach, Asian greens or lettuce as well as herbs like basil or chocolate mint – and sometimes I swap out the avo' for fruit like mango or peaches. You could use nut butter instead of nuts here and it would work just as well.

---

1 frozen banana, peeled

½ avocado, stone removed

1 large handful leafy greens and herbs (such as kale, basil, spinach or parsley)

2 teaspoons chia seeds

1 teaspoon maca powder (optional)

1 date, pitted (optional)

3 tablespoons cashew nuts or 1 tablespoon of nut butter

200 ml (7 fl oz) almond milk

Put all the ingredients into a blender and blitz on high speed until smooth. Check the consistency – if it's looking a little too thick add a splash of water to loosen the mixture – then pour into a glass and enjoy.

TIP *Remember to peel your bananas before you freeze them – it's far less fuss at this point and means they will be ready to blitz.*

Pictured on page 24

Fresh juice

EACH SERVES 1

MRS Though we love having fresh juices in the morning we're not so in love with cleaning the juicer, so we don't have these every day. When we do, we like to combine lots of lovely fruit, vegetables and herbs to make bright, colourful juices. Here's a few of our favourites ...

2 oranges, peeled and cut into chunks

¼ pineapple, peeled and cut into chunks

2 carrots, cut into chunks

2 cm (¾ in) piece fresh ginger, cut into chunks

Orange

Put the orange, pineapple, carrot and ginger pieces through the juicer, switching between fruits as you go so you end up with a nicely mixed juice. Pour into a glass and drink up.

4 kale leaves

1 small handful parsley

1 small handful mint

2 green apples, cored and cut into chunks

1 celery stalk, cut into chunks

1 Lebanese (short) cucumber, cut into chunks

Green

Before turning it on, pop the kale leaves, parsley and mint into the juicer followed by the apple (this will help push everything through). Start juicing, adding the celery stalk and cucumber, and alternating between pieces, then pour into a glass and enjoy.

1 small handful mint

2 beetroot (beets), cut into chunks

2 red apples, cored and cut into chunks

2 carrots, cut into chunks

Red

Before turning it on, pop the mint leaves into the juicer followed by the beetroot (this will help push the mint through). Start juicing, adding the apples and carrots and alternating between pieces, then pour into a glass and enjoy.

Pictured on page 25

Pot-set yoghurt

MAKES 1 LITRE (34 FL OZ/4 CUPS)

MR Yoghurt is so cheap and easy to make – just add your own vanilla or blitzed fruit to make flavoured ones for the kids or yourself. I usually pop this in at night after the oven has been on at dinner, then take it out the next morning.

800 ml (27 fl oz) full-fat homogenised organic or biodynamic milk

80 g (2¾ oz) organic natural yoghurt

Add the milk to a large saucepan over a medium–low heat and warm, stirring occasionally, until the milk has reached 90°C (194°F) when tested with a sugar thermometer, or when you can see lots of small bubbles start to come up the side of the pot.

Pour the milk into a cold bowl and leave to stand until cooled to 36–37°C (97–99°F), or the point at which you can comfortably hold your finger in it as though it were a nice, warm bath. Stir in the yoghurt, then transfer to a 1 litre (34 fl oz/4 cups) sterilised jar and seal with a lid.

Preheat the oven to 250°C (480°F/Gas 9).

Place the jar in an ovenproof stockpot or other suitable container and top it up with water until it reaches the level of the yoghurt mixture. Carefully transfer to the oven, then turn off the heat and leave for 10 hours, or overnight, until set.

Once set, transfer the jar to the fridge and keep for up to 2 weeks.

TIP *Once you've made this, remember to set aside 80 g (2¾ oz) of the yoghurt to make your next batch – that way you'll never have to buy yoghurt again!*

Natural muesli

MAKES APPROX. 750 G (SERVES 8)

MRS I've never been a fan of boxed cereals, so it was a revelation when I realised I could combine all the ingredients we already had in our cupboard to make a brilliant muesli. Feel free to swap out any of the ingredients here for others you may have in your cupboard ... cranberries, dried apricots, pistachio nuts and almonds would all work well. Also, remember that old nuts and seeds will taste stale, so buy these in small amounts and use them regularly to ensure you have a fresh mixture.

350 g (12½ oz/3½ cups) rolled (porridge) oats

100 g (3½ oz) sultanas (golden raisins)

60 g (2 oz) dried pear slices, finely chopped

50 g (1¾ oz) coconut flakes

50 g (1¾ oz) chia seeds

50 g (1¾ oz/ ⅓ cup) pepitas (pumpkin seeds)

30 g (1 oz) sesame seeds

100 g (3½ oz/ ⅔ cup) cashew nuts

Mix all the ingredients together in a large bowl, then transfer to an airtight container or jar and store for up to 1 month. Serve with your choice of milk and fresh seasonal or poached fruits.

Pancakes – thin or fat

MAKES 4

> **MR** I cook pancakes for the boys on weekends – it's our little Saturday treat and I get them to count down from five when I go to flip them in the pan. It's fun. The difference between fat or thin pancakes here is simply whether you use self-raising flour or plain, with the self-raising giving a more American-style thick pancake and the plain a more French-style crêpe.

150 g (5½ oz/1 cup) plain (all-purpose) or self-raising flour

1½ tablespoons sugar

1 free-range egg

185–250 ml (6–8½ fl oz/ ¾–1 cup) milk (185 ml/ 6 fl oz/ ¾ cup) if using self-raising flour)

2 teaspoons ghee or unsalted butter

Mix the flour and sugar together in a bowl and make a well in the centre. Crack the egg into the well and whisk together to combine, then slowly add the milk, whisking continuously, until all the milk has been incorporated and you have a smooth, lump-free batter.

Heat a large frying pan over a high heat. Melt ½ teaspoon of the ghee in the pan, then ladle in a quarter of the mixture. Cook for 1 minute until lightly golden, then flip the pancake over and cook for a further minute. Remove from the pan and set aside on a plate, then repeat with the remaining ghee and pancake mixture. Serve immediately with your topping of choice. (I like mine with bananas and maple syrup, Finn with jam and Jay with Promite. Yuck.)

A NOTE ON HONEY FROM MATT ...
Honey is the original sweetener and was used for centuries before refined sugar beet or sugar-cane came along. It is essentially made up of glucose, sucrose and fructose sugars in differing ratios depending on where and what plant species the bees that produced the honey were foraging on, these differences giving it its many distinct flavours. I like to buy local honey – not least because many imports are diluted with sugar syrups to save money – and get mine from my good friends Mat and Vanessa of Rooftop Honey, who are doing amazing things for bees and honey in Melbourne's CBD and suburbs. As honey is what the bees live off during the colder months when there is no nectar, it's good practice to make sure that the beekeeper you buy yours from does not rob too much honey out of the hive. Personally I don't like robust, bold-flavoured honeys, preferring the softer tones of wildflower and clover.

Nonna Leah's tomato smash

SERVES 4

> **MRS** My Mum – a.k.a. Nonna Leah – always puts a big bowl of this on the breakfast table on Christmas day morning, usually with poached free-range eggs, toast and Aberdeen sausage (some of you will know what that is, but for those who don't, it's similar to meatloaf).

1 tablespoon extra-virgin olive oil

1 red onion, sliced

1 × 400 g (14 oz) tin chopped tomatoes

1 teaspoon curry powder

1 tablespoon tomato sauce (ketchup)

1 tablespoon worcestershire sauce

1 teaspoon sugar

½ teaspoon salt flakes

1 teaspoon cornflour (cornstarch)

poached free-range eggs, toast, to serve

Heat the olive oil in a saucepan over a medium heat, add the onion and sauté until soft, about 5 minutes. Add the chopped tomatoes, curry powder, tomato and worcestershire sauces, sugar, salt and water and mix together well, then bring to the boil, cover with a lid and cook for 2–3 minutes. Remove the lid, reduce the heat and simmer for 5 minutes, until the mixture has thickened and reduced slightly and the flavours have melded together.

Mix the cornflour together with a few tablespoons of water to make a paste, then add it to the tomato mix. Stir everything together well and return to the boil, then remove from the heat and leave to sit until ready to serve.

Porridge

Mum's version

SERVES 1–2

MRS This is a staple breakfast for the colder months. I have memories of my Mum cooking porridge for me as a kid in winter and, just as I started to get sick of eating it, the weather would warm up again and we would give it up until the next winter.

100 g (3½ oz/1 cup) rolled (porridge) oats

pinch of salt flakes

25 g (1 oz) sultanas (golden raisins)

1 tablespoon pepitas (pumpkin seeds)

1 tablespoon coconut flakes

1 banana, peeled and thinly sliced

100 ml (3½ fl oz) milk (whatever type you prefer)

honey, to serve (optional)

Add the oats, 500 ml (17 fl oz/2 cups) water and salt to a small saucepan over a medium–low heat and cook for 7–8 minutes, stirring occasionally, until the oats are just starting to turn creamy. Stir through the sultanas, adding a splash of water from the kettle if the porridge starts to stick to the bottom of the pan, then remove from the heat and spoon into bowls.

To serve, sprinkle over the pepitas and coconut flakes, top with the banana slices and pour over your choice of milk, drizzling over a little honey if you like things sweeter. Tuck in.

Porridge

Dad's version

SERVES 1

MR Ok, so our kids prefer their Mum's porridge. But my version is how I remember it as a kid and I'm pretty sure it's how Goldilocks liked it. So there.

75 g (2¾ oz/ ¾ cup) rolled (porridge) oats

tiny pinch of salt flakes

125 ml (4 fl oz/ ½ cup) milk, plus extra to serve

2½ teaspoons sugar

The night before you want to eat the porridge, put the oats in a bowl and cover with the 250 ml (8½ fl oz/ 1 cup) water. Leave to soak overnight.

The next morning, strain the excess water from the oats and rinse lightly, then transfer to a large saucepan together with the salt and half the milk. Cook over a high heat, stirring occasionally, for 3–4 minutes or until the milk has been absorbed, then stir in the rest of the milk and continue to cook until nicely warmed through.

Pour into a bowl, tip a little cold milk over the top and sprinkle over the sugar to serve.

Green eggs

SERVES 1

1 large handful baby spinach leaves

1 handful soft herbs (parsley, mint, chervil)

2 free-range eggs

pinch of salt flakes

pinch of freshly grated nutmeg

1 tablespoon extra-virgin olive oil

50 g (1¾ oz) goat's cheese or feta, crumbled

buttered toast, to serve

Preheat the oven to 180°C (350°F/Gas 4).

Throw the spinach, herbs, eggs, salt and nutmeg into a food processor and blitz for 20 seconds to combine.

Heat the olive oil in an ovenproof frying pan over a medium heat. Pour the green egg mixture into the hot pan and use a spatula to bring in the set edges, letting the liquid mix run out to the side of the pan again. Scatter the goat's cheese or feta over the eggs and cook for 2 minutes until the bottom is set.

Transfer the pan to the oven and leave to cook for 8–10 minutes, or until the eggs are cooked through. Remove from the oven and serve immediately in the pan with toast on the side. I like to eat mine with sauerkraut or sweet chilli jam.

Lunchboxes

MRS I actually love making lunchboxes in the morning, whether for myself or the kids. If you think about it, lunchboxes can be a part of our lives for a long time – from that first day at school right through our working lives until retirement – so this section is very much for kids and adults alike. When Finn started at school this year, we asked him what his favourite things were in his first week and he said playing with his friends and Mumma making his lunches. That kid!

I always made my lunch for school as a kid and pretty much always had the same thing – a few sandwiches, some bickies, a frozen juice box and an apple. Cold pizza or spinach and feta pie were very much treats to be added in when we had leftovers and, although I was envious of the kids whose lunchboxes contained chips and cheese sticks, little did I know my Mum was teaching us an appreciation for real food that would stick with me all my life.

It's really hard to get vegetables into kids' lunchboxes, particularly when you eat seasonally, but it can be done – I aim for fruit, a snack, a sweet thing and a main 'lunch' as the basic setup and try and get some veggies in there somehow. It's also really hard to get enough variety, but I have found that the boys are pretty happy with a weekly rotation, which means I cook up a few goodies for the lunchbox on a Sunday (see Sunday Baking Sessions, page 84) and keep it consistent for the week before changing it up the following week. And speaking of changing it up, don't feel restricted to just the recipes in this chapter either, as there are lots of other great recipes in this book that are lunchbox friendly – quesadillas, wraps, chicken noodle salad and zucchini bread can all be made up easily in the morning and are sturdy enough to be transported without problems.

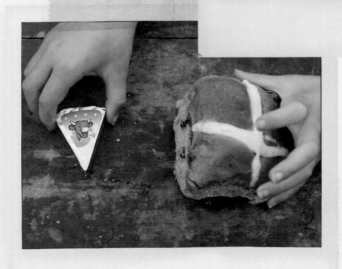

Zucchini & feta fritters

MAKES 12

> **MRS** These are a go-to dish to have on hand in the fridge for filling up lunchboxes or for making quick lunches at home – just add a salad and a dipping sauce and you're away. They can be varied almost endlessly – the zucchini substituted for other veg like grated carrots or potato, the feta switched for something like haloumi or mozzarella and the mint replaced with any fresh herb you happen to have on hand or growing in the garden. I like to double up the recipe and cook a load, then freeze the excess in batches for a later date.

2 small–medium zucchini (courgettes), coarsely grated

150 g (5½ oz/1 cup) feta, crumbled

10–12 mint leaves, finely chopped

1 free-range egg, beaten

70 g (2½ oz) plain (all-purpose) flour

1 teaspoon baking powder

2 teaspoons cornflour (cornstarch)

½ teaspoon ground cumin

½ teaspoon salt flakes

3–4 tablespoons extra-virgin olive oil

cucumber yoghurt, to serve (see tip)

Squeeze out the grated zucchini over the sink to remove any excess moisture, then transfer to a large bowl. Add the feta and mint and mix together well. Stir in the beaten egg, then add the dry ingredients a little at a time, stirring with a fork as you go, until well combined.

Heat 1 tablespoon olive oil in a large frying pan over a medium heat. Add tablespoonfuls of the fritter mixture to the pan to form 3–4 rounds each about 7 cm (2¾ in) in diameter. Cook for 3 minutes on each side until lightly golden, then remove from the pan, place on paper towel and cover with a tea towel (dish towel) to keep warm. Repeat with the remaining batter, adding another tablespoon of olive oil to the pan with each batch.

Leave the fritters to cool completely before packing up into airtight containers ready for popping into lunchboxes or the fridge, where they will keep for up to 3 days.

TIP *CUCUMBER YOGHURT*
We like to serve these with a simple yoghurt and cucumber dip. To make it, stir together 3 tablespoons natural yoghurt, 1 grated Lebanese (short) cucumber, 5 chopped mint leaves and a pinch of salt flakes in a small bowl.

Pictured on page 45

Pirate cookies

MAKES 24

MRS We call these pirate cookies as the freckles look like colourful treasure. They are seriously easy, though because they are so simple it's worth hunting out good-quality flour and butter to use here as you will notice the difference (and try not to use flour that has been sitting in the cupboard for the past year untouched). You could substitute the freckles for any other sweets (candy) that can withstand the baking time, and if you don't have coconut flour to hand, just add the same quantity of plain flour instead.

180 g (6½ oz) unsalted butter, at room temperature

165 g (6 oz/ ¾ cup) raw (demerara) sugar

1 free-range egg

1 teaspoon vanilla paste

225 g (8 oz/1½ cups) plain (all-purpose) flour

35 g (1¼ oz/ ¼ cup) coconut flour

1 heaped teaspoon baking powder

24 chocolate freckles, to decorate

Preheat the oven to 180°C (350°F/Gas 4). Line two baking trays with baking paper.

Using an electric mixer, beat the butter and sugar together in a mixing bowl until creamy. Add the egg and vanilla paste and continue to beat until light and fluffy, then stir in the flours and baking powder with a wooden spoon, adding a little at a time, to form a dough (it will be quite a dry one, so you'll need some muscle power to stir everything together!).

Scoop out a teaspoonful of the cookie dough and roll it into a ball, then place it on one of the prepared baking trays. Place a freckle on the top of the ball and press down to flatten it slightly. Repeat with the remaining dough and freckles, leaving 5 cm (2 in) space in between each to allow room for the cookies to spread.

Bake the cookies for 15 minutes or until lightly golden. Remove from the oven and leave to cool on a wire rack before eating. Keep stored in an airtight container for up to 5–7 days.

TIP *I usually only cook half of the dough when I make these; the remainder of the dough I push into a sausage shape and roll well in baking paper, then put in the freezer. When I need more cookies, I slice them off the roll with a hot knife and bake from frozen. Just add the freckle once the dough has started to soften in the oven.*

Pictured on page 45

Salami scrolls

MAKES 8

> **MRS** The boys love salami and this is a fun recipe we can make together. If you don't rate salami then you could always use ham or pastrami instead. Alternatively, blitz up some semi-dried tomatoes with a fresh tomato and spread this over the pastry, then sprinkle over some feta and basil leaves and you have a rather delicious vegetarian version.

1 frozen butter puff pastry sheet, thawed

60 g (2 oz) thin salami slices

100 g (3½ oz) asiago cheese, grated (you could use cheddar)

30 g (1 oz) salted butter, melted

Preheat the oven to 180°C (350°F/Gas 4). Line a baking tray with baking paper.

Lay the puff pastry sheet out onto a clean work surface and arrange the salami slices evenly over to cover, leaving a 2 cm (¾ in) border at the top edge. Sprinkle the cheese all over the salami then, taking the bottom edge of the pastry sheet, roll it up into a tight, long cylinder to the border at the top. Brush the exposed pastry with a little melted butter, then continue to roll the pastry up to seal everything together. Brush the rolled pastry cylinder all over with a little more melted butter, place it on the prepared baking tray and transfer to the fridge for 10 minutes to firm up.

Once firmed, remove the pastry cylinder from the fridge and slice it into eight rounds. Arrange the scrolls cut-side up on the baking tray, making sure they are closely packed together (this will ensure they keep their shape). Brush the top of the scrolls with the remaining melted butter and bake for 30 minutes until golden brown. Remove from the oven and transfer to a wire rack to cool.

TIP *We like to make a big batch of these scrolls and freeze the rest for later, defrosting them thoroughly when needed and flashing them in the oven at 180°C (350°F/Gas 4) for 7 minutes just before serving.*

Pictured on page 44

Chocolate & beetroot muffins

MAKES 8

> **MRS** The hooligans love chocolate so much that the beetroot here doesn't get a second thought. It also adds a lovely sweetness and the olive oil keeps the muffins moist. I use cacao powder but you can use drinking chocolate instead if that's what you have in the cupboard – it will just make the muffins a little bit sweeter.

1 beetroot (beet), about 200 g (7 oz)

2 free-range eggs

80 ml (2½ fl oz/ ⅓ cup) extra-virgin olive oil

110 g (4 oz/ ½ cup) raw (demerara) sugar

150 g (5½ oz/1 cup) plain (all-purpose) flour

2 teaspoons baking powder

30 g (1 oz/ ¼ cup) raw cacao powder or drinking chocolate

1 teaspoon vanilla paste

pinch of salt flakes

Put the beetroot in a saucepan and cover with cold water, then bring to the boil and cook for about 35 minutes, or until the beetroot is easily pierced with the point of a sharp knife. Remove from the water and leave to cool for 10 minutes before using a paper towel to rub off the skin (it's easier to do this while the beetroot is still slightly warm). Transfer to a food processor and blitz to a chunky paste.

Preheat the oven to 180°C (350°F/Gas 4). Line a regular muffin tin with muffin cases.

Beat the eggs, olive oil and sugar together in an electric mixer for 2–3 minutes, until thick and creamy. Fold in the beetroot purée then gradually mix in the flour, baking powder, cacao powder, vanilla paste and salt.

Spoon the batter into the muffin cases about 2 cm (¾ in) from the top and bake for 25–30 minutes, or until the muffins are firm to the touch. Set aside on a wire rack to cool, storing any that aren't eaten straight away in an airtight container in the fridge where they will keep for up to 2–3 days.

TIP *I usually cook the beetroot the night before so it's ready to use in the morning to bake, transferring the purée to an airtight container and storing it in the fridge until needed.*

Pictured on page 44

Sausage rolls

MAKES 24

MRS Who doesn't love a sausage roll? These ones are especially good and have the added advantage of sneaking some vegetables into the lunchbox, though you can always leave out the carrot if you prefer. Our number one freezer essential is puff pastry sheets, so they are always on hand. Make sure you get the good stuff made with butter.

500 g (1 lb 2 oz) free-range minced (ground) pork

1 carrot, grated

1 teaspoon ground cumin

1 teaspoon dried oregano

pinch of salt flakes

pinch of freshly ground black pepper

1 free-range egg, beaten

2 frozen butter puff pastry sheets, thawed

50 g (1¾ oz) melted unsalted butter

2 teaspoons sesame seeds (optional)

Preheat the oven to 180°C (350°F/Gas 4) and line two baking trays with baking paper.

Add the pork, carrot, cumin, oregano, salt and pepper to a bowl. Use your hands to mix everything together well, then add the egg and mix again.

Lay the puff pastry sheets out onto a clean work surface and slice them in half lengthways to form four equal-sized rectangles. You will be making four long rolls, so divide the mince into four parts and work on each roll separately. Transfer one part of the mince to a pastry rectangle and squish with your hands to form a long roll the length of the long edge of the pastry sheet. Brush the uncovered pastry with melted butter then roll it up tightly to enclose the filling. Repeat with the rest of the minced pork mix and the other three pastry rectangles.

Brush all over the outside of the pastry rolls with a little more melted butter and sprinkle with sesame seeds, if using. Slice each roll into six pieces.

Arrange the sausage rolls on the prepared baking tray and bake for 30 minutes, until the pastry is golden and flaky and the meat is cooked through. Leave to cool on wire racks before packing up into lunchboxes (extras can be stored in the fridge for up to 2 days).

Pictured on page 50

Banana cake

MAKES 1 CAKE

> **MRS** We always have bananas hanging around in the kitchen. When they start to get ripe I either pop them in the freezer for smoothies or I make a banana cake like this for school lunches, baking it in a square tin to make it easy for cutting and portioning up into lunchboxes. Sometimes I use spelt flour instead of self-raising and add baking powder too, or I throw in a handful of choc chips.

100 g (3½ oz) unsalted butter

110 g (4 oz/ ½ cup) raw (demerara) sugar

2 free-range eggs

1 teaspoon vanilla paste

3 really ripe bananas, peeled and mashed

200 g (7 oz/1⅓ cups) self-raising flour, sifted

¼ teaspoon bicarbonate of soda (baking soda)

80 ml (2½ fl oz/ ⅓ cup) milk

Preheat the oven to 180°C (350°F/Gas 4). Grease and line a 20 x 20 cm (8 x 8 in) cake tin.

Beat the butter and sugar together in a bowl with an electric mixer until really light and fluffy, then add the eggs one at a time, beating well in between. Add the vanilla and bananas and continue to beat on slow speed until combined.

Sift over the flour and bicarbonate of soda and stir into the mixture, then pour over the milk and mix together to form a slightly runny batter. Pour into the prepared tin and bake for 40–50 minutes, or until lightly golden on top and a skewer inserted into the centre of the cake comes out clean. Leave to cool slightly in the tin for 5 minutes, then turn onto a wire rack and leave to cool completely. Transfer the cake to a large tin and keep it on the side, cutting off pieces as needed.

Pictured on page 50

Frittata muffins

MAKES 6

MRS These are the best use of left-over vegetables ever. And those veg could be roast potatoes and carrots, steamed green beans, cauliflower or broccoli or sautéed mushrooms ... it doesn't matter really, just as long as they are already cooked. If you had some meat you could use that as well, like cooked sausages, bacon, meatballs or roast chicken. I quite often make these at breakfast time when we have a surplus of eggs and no bread for sandwiches for lunch. They take no time to prep and are cooked while I am nagging the hooligans to get dressed ... again!

180 g (6½ oz) left-over cooked vegetables, cut into 1 cm (½ in) cubes

180 g (6½ oz) cheese (goat's cheese, cream cheese, feta, cheddar etc.), cut into 1 cm (½ in) cubes

4 free-range eggs

60 ml (2 fl oz/ ¼ cup) milk

good pinch of salt flakes

1 handful soft herbs (such as parsley, chives, tarragon, basil and mint), chopped (optional)

Preheat the oven to 180°C (350°F/Gas 4) and line a 6-cup muffin tin with 15 x 15 cm (6 x 6 in) squares of baking paper.

Divide the cooked vegetable and cheese pieces between the muffin holes.

Whisk the eggs, milk and salt together in a bowl until well combined. Stir in the herbs, if using, then pour the egg mixture evenly into the lined muffin holes, giving the tin a little shake to make sure the mix finds its way around the fillings evenly.

Bake for 20 minutes, or until the egg mixture is cooked through and firm with no wobbly bits. Remove from the oven and leave to cool in the tin before packing into lunchboxes (extras can be stored in the fridge for 1–2 days).

Pictured on page 51

Pumpkin scones

MAKES 10

60 g (2 oz) raw (demerara) sugar

60 g (2 oz/ ⅓ cup) unsalted butter

1 free-range egg

150 g (5½ oz) cooked pumpkin (squash), mashed

300 g (10½ oz) self-raising flour, plus extra for dusting

pinch of salt flakes

milk, for brushing

butter and jam, to serve

Preheat the oven to 210°C (410°F/Gas 6½). Dust a baking tray lightly with flour.

Cream the sugar and butter together in a bowl until light and fluffy, then add the egg and beat well. Stir in the pumpkin with a wooden spoon to combine, then add the flour and salt, little by little, to form a dough.

Using your hands, pat the dough out on a floured bench to a thickness of 2–3 cm (¾–1¼ in), then use a floured 6 cm (2 ½ in) cookie cutter (or a thin-rimmed glass if you don't have one like me) to cut out individual scones.

Transfer the scones to the floured baking tray, brush the tops with a little milk and bake for 10–12 minutes until lightly golden. Leave to cool on a wire rack before serving with butter and jam.

Pictured on page 51

Lunch

MR Why does lunch always play second fiddle to other meals? I find it strange how little effort, care and time people give it. As young children all we really want to do is eat it as quickly as possible and get back to playing. As teenagers those packed lunches are thrown away on the way home so Mum thinks you've eaten them, or there's the lunch money for the cafeteria that gets kept to be spent on something else. From there it's on to grabbing lunch on the run or wolfing down that quick bite at your desk. Why and when did this happen?

Thank goodness for retirement, I say. At least then there seems to be time to process, slow down and, well ... eat lunch properly.

Sadly, all this rushing around means that we treat lunch as though it's the middle child nobody really cares about (particularly in comparison to dinner) and we spend far less money and effort on it as a result, even though it deserves just the same amount of thought as every other meal we eat. No matter where it comes from a sandwich should always be fresh, delicious and made from quality, well-sourced ingredients, for example, as should the soup, pie, salad, rice paper rolls, sushi and all the other quick lunch meals we treat as staples. Yet for some reason we allow ourselves to say, 'Oh, it wasn't that good but that's ok, it's just lunch.'

It wasn't always like this. In ages past, lunch used to be the main event, while even today some European countries like to take a long lunch and then have a sleep afterwards. Legends, I say! In this chapter we have tried to give this put-upon meal back some of its lost importance by sharing some of our favourite and most delicious recipes for it. Anyway, that's enough talking from me, it's time for you to turn the page and get stuck in – let's do lunch.

Double cheese quesadillas

MAKES 2

> **MRS** We eat these so often that Finn told me one day, 'Mum, I don't want quesadillas, I just want plain toast'. The grated cheese here is the base filling but everything else can be mixed up as you like.

4 flour tortillas

185 g (6½ oz/1½ cups) grated cheese (use two types like cheddar, asiago, manchego or mozzarella)

1 long sweet yellow capsicum (bell pepper), seeded and sliced (optional)

2 coriander (cilantro) sprigs, leaves stripped (optional)

TO SERVE (OPTIONAL)

avocado, smashed

natural yoghurt

sauerkraut

sweet chilli jam

Heat a large frying pan over a medium heat.

Lay two of the tortillas on a clean work surface. Divide the grated cheese, peppers and coriander, if using, evenly between them, then top with the remaining tortillas.

Add one of the quesadillas to the frying pan and cook for 2 minutes on each side until lightly browned and the cheese has melted. Remove from the pan and cut into 6–8 wedges, then repeat with the remaining quesadilla.

Can be served with smashed avocado, yoghurt, sauerkraut and sweet chilli jam.

TIP *While pretty much anything can work inside a tortilla, a few of our favourite fillings are: salami and semi-dried tomatoes; roast chicken, feta and basil; baked beans and bacon; roast pumpkin and pesto.*

Silverbeet & feta filo triangles

MAKES 18

MRS My Mum taught me how to cook spinach and feta pie as a teenager and it has remained a favourite to this day. It always gets tweaked as we make it, with additions like grated nutmeg or pine nuts. Making the pie into triangles was a revelation as you can bake and freeze them in advance, then warm them through in a moderate oven for 15–20 minutes when needed.

20 ml (¾ fl oz) extra-virgin olive oil

700 g (1 lb 9 oz) (1 large bunch) silverbeet (Swiss chard), stalks removed and roughly chopped

1 leek, white and light green part only, halved and thinly sliced

good pinch of freshly grated nutmeg

good pinch of salt flakes

200 g (7 oz) feta, crumbled

50 g (1¾ oz) cream cheese

2 free-range eggs, beaten

12 filo pastry sheets

50 g (1¾ oz) salted butter, melted

TIP *We make a white version and replace the silverbeet and leek with 1 cauliflower and 1 onion. Blitz them in a food processor and combine them (raw) with the remaining ingredients, then continue as per the method.*

Preheat the oven to 180°C (350°F/Gas 4) and line two baking trays with baking paper.

Heat the olive oil in a large frying pan over a medium heat, add the silverbeet, leek, nutmeg and salt and sauté until the veggies have softened, about 3 minutes. Remove from the heat, transfer to a mixing bowl with the feta, cream cheese and eggs, and mix everything together well.

Lay one filo pastry sheet out onto a floured work surface with the short edges at the top and bottom and brush with a little of the melted butter. Lay a second sheet on top and brush again with butter. Cut the sheets with a sharp knife from top to bottom lengthways into three equal-sized strips. Move the strips slightly apart.

Place a tablespoon of the filling at the bottom left-hand side of one strip, then fold it up on a diagonal to meet the right edge and make a triangle. Fold the triangle up and align with the right side. Fold the triangle again on the diagonal to meet the left side, then up again to align with the left side. Continue to fold until you have reached the end of the pastry strip. Brush the triangle all over with melted butter to seal it tightly and place it on one of the prepared baking trays. Continue with the remaining pastry sheets and filling mixture, brushing the sheets with melted butter as you go, until all the filling has been used and you are left with 18 filled triangles.

Bake the filo triangles in the oven for 20 minutes, or until crisp and golden. Serve warm with a Greek-style salad of cucumber, tomatoes and feta.

Hawaiian pizza

MAKES 2 LARGE PIZZAS OR 3 MEDIUM PIZZAS

MRS This is controversial but it's just not a pizza if it doesn't have pineapple on it in our household. This is a good weekend activity – we like to make the dough in the morning and roll the bases out for lunch, with the boys putting their own toppings on their pizzas.

4 teaspoons dried yeast

2 teaspoons sugar

600 g (1 lb 5 oz/4 cups) plain (all-purpose) flour

2 teaspoons salt flakes

3 tablespoons extra-virgin olive oil

30 g (1 oz/ ¼ cup) semolina

TOPPINGS

90 g (3 oz) tomato paste (concentrated purée)

2 teaspoons dried oregano

200 g (7 oz) free-range ham, roughly chopped

⅓ pineapple, skin removed and roughly chopped

200 g (7 oz/1⅓ cups) grated mozzarella

Pour 375 ml (12½ fl oz/1½ cups) water into a measuring cup, add the yeast and sugar and leave for 5 minutes for the yeast to activate (you can tell that it's working as the surface of the water will become all foamy).

Place the flour and salt in a large bowl and pour over the yeast mixture and olive oil. Mix everything together with your hands to form a dough, then tip it out onto a floured work surface. Knead the dough for 10 minutes until it has changed from crumbly to smooth and elastic, then pop it in a floured bowl, cover it with a tea towel (dish towel) and keep it in the warmest part of the kitchen for 30 minutes, or until doubled in size.

Preheat the oven to 210°C (410°F/Gas 6½) and sprinkle two baking trays with semolina (this will stop your bases from sticking to the trays).

Once the dough has risen, punch it down to remove any large air bubbles and knead it again for another minute, then divide it in half. Keeping one half covered, roll out the other on a floured bench into a rough circle about 30 cm (12 in) in diameter (don't worry if it isn't perfectly round – ours never are). Transfer the pizza base to one of the prepared baking trays, then repeat with the remaining dough.

Spread the tomato paste over the pizza bases, then sprinkle over the oregano, top with the ham and pineapple and scatter over the grated mozzarella to finish. Bake for 15 minutes, or until the cheese is golden brown and the bases are nicely crispy. Serve immediately with a green salad.

Chicken & miso noodle salad

SERVES 2

> **MR** I like to whip up this quick, simple lunch salad from time to time when I'm in a rush (the poached chicken can be made up in advance and refrigerated until needed). It's very flexible and you can pretty much use anything you have to hand, really, swapping the chicken for salmon, tinned tuna, sautéed beef or pork or taking the meat out all together and adding more veggies like beans, broccoli or peas.

1 × 200 g (7 oz) free-range boneless, skinless chicken breast

180 g (6½ oz) soba noodles

1 cucumber, diced

1 carrot, cut into thin strips or grated

3 spring onions (scallions), sliced

salt flakes and freshly ground black pepper

chilli sauce, to serve (optional)

DRESSING

1 tablespoon togarashi (Japanese chilli spice blend)

1½ tablespoons red miso paste

1 teaspoon white sesame seeds

2 tablespoons mirin

2 tablespoons soy sauce

2 tablespoons rice vinegar

75 ml (2½ fl oz) non-GMO vegetable oil

Bring 500 ml (17 fl oz/2 cups) water to the boil in a saucepan. Add the chicken breast, reduce the heat and simmer gently for 6 minutes, then remove the pan from the heat and leave the chicken to poach for 15 minutes, or until the liquid is cool enough for you to remove the meat with your fingers. Dice the chicken breast and set aside.

To make the dressing, mix together the togarashi, miso and sesame seeds in a small bowl until combined. Whisk in the mirin, soy sauce and rice vinegar then lightly whisk in the oil.

Cook the soba noodles in a saucepan of boiling water as per the packet instructions, rinse under cold water and add to a large mixing bowl together with the poached chicken and all the other ingredients. Pour over the dressing and mix together thoroughly, then leave to sit for 3 minutes to allow the noodles to absorb all the flavours. Season to taste and serve with a little chilli sauce, if you like (I do).

TIP *For extra flavour, try adding aromatics like herbs and spices or citrus rind to the poaching liquid (which can also be kept and used later as chicken stock). Togarashi is a Japanese spice mixture available at good Asian supermarkets and specialty stores – if you don't have any to hand you can always swap in an all-purpose pepper seasoning instead.*

Flatbreads with salads & spreads

MAKES 8 BREADS (SERVES 2–4)

> **M R** These flatbreads make an excellent simple lunch with one or two salads and some spreads laid out in the middle of the table. Depending on how I'm feeling (and the weather) sometimes I cook them on the barbecue, or at other times on a grill plate or baked on the pizza stone in the oven. They also go brilliantly with any type of curry like the ones on pages 178 and page 217.

2 teaspoons dried yeast

300 g (10½ oz/2 cups) plain (all-purpose) flour

140 g (5 oz) Greek-style yoghurt

3 tablespoons milk

1 tablespoon non-GMO vegetable oil

pinch of salt flakes

1 teaspoon ras el hanout

TO SERVE

Hummus (page 78)

Harissa (page 245)

Cucumber yoghurt (page 40)

For the flatbreads, add 2 tablespoons lukewarm water and yeast to a small bowl, stir together and leave for 5 minutes for the yeast to activate.

Put the yeast mixture into a large bowl together with all the remaining ingredients and mix everything together using your hands to form a firm dough (alternatively, put everything into a mixer with the dough hook attachment added).

Cover the bowl with a tea towel (dish towel) and leave the dough to sit for 30–40 minutes in a warm place to rise.

While the flatbreads are rising, make up your salad (or salads) and sides of choice.

Once the dough has risen, knock it back on a lightly floured surface. Divide the dough into 8 equal-sized pieces and roll each out into thin long breads, then transfer them to floured baking trays and leave them to rise again for another 30–40 minutes.

To cook the flatbreads, place them on a hot barbecue or chargrill pan and cook for 1–3 minutes on each side, turning with tongs, until puffed up and charred all over. Alternatively, transfer them to a pizza stone and bake for 7 minutes in an oven preheated to 240°C (480°F/Gas 9) until golden.

To serve, arrange the flatbreads on the centre of the table with your choice of salads and spreads.

SALAD ONE

½ bunch flat-leaf (Italian) parsley, torn

½ bunch mint, torn

1 shallot, sliced

3 cucumber pickles, sliced

juice of 1 lemon

1 tablespoon dukkah

2 tablespoons extra-virgin olive oil

salt flakes

Put everything into a bowl and mix well.

SALAD TWO

5 vine ripened tomatoes, cut into chunks

1 cucumber, diced

1 teaspoon sumac

freshly ground black pepper

2 tablespoons red-wine vinegar

2 tablespoons extra-virgin olive oil

Put everything into a bowl and mix well.

SALAD THREE

3 tablespoons extra-virgin olive oil

1 small eggplant, diced, salted for 2 minutes and rinsed

1 small red onion, diced

2 tablespoons Mr Wilkinson's kasundi (page 239)

1 tablespoon natural yoghurt

½ bunch coriander (cilantro), roughly chopped

Heat the olive oil in a medium saucepan over a high heat. Fry the egglant and onion until golden. Mix in the kasundi then pour into a serving bowl. Mix in the yogurt and herbs to serve.

SALAD FOUR

2 zucchini (courgettes)

pinch of salt flakes

100 g (3½ oz) Danish-style feta

2 tablespoons sultanas (golden raisins)

¼ bunch mint, torn

2 teaspoons toasted pine nuts

Slice the zucchini into thin ribbons and transfer to a colander. Sprinkle with salt and leave for 2 minutes, then rinse and dry. Add to a bowl with all the remaining ingredients and mix well.

SALAD FIVE

250 g (9 oz) minced (ground) lamb or beef

1 tablespoon ras el hanout

1 red onion, finely diced

½ teaspoon salt flakes

½ teaspoon sumac

1 tablespoon pine nuts

1 tablespoon pomegranate molasses

2 tablespoons red-wine vinegar

2 tablespoons extra-virgin olive oil

30 g (1 oz/ ½ cup) chopped mint

30 g (1 oz/ ½ cup) chopped parsley

Mix together all the ingredients in a bowl. Heat a large frying pan over a high heat, add the lamb mixture and sauté for 7–8 minutes, or until the meat is browned on all sides and cooked through. Tip into a bowl and set aside to cool.

Pictured on pages 66–67

Tomato & red lentil soup

SERVES 2

> **MRS** I love to make this soup when I am at home working by myself, freezing the second portion for next time around. It's a one-pot wonder – chop up the carrot and celery (or whatever veg you happen to have handy), throw it all in the pan and in 30 minutes it's done.

1 tablespoon extra-virgin olive oil

1 carrot, finely diced

1 celery stalk, finely diced

1 teaspoon ground cumin

1 teaspoon ground coriander

½ teaspoon ground turmeric

125 g (4½ oz / ½ cup) dried red lentils

500 ml (17 fl oz/2 cups) water or vegetable stock

1 × 400 g (14 oz) tin chopped tomatoes

1 teaspoon apple-cider vinegar

salt flakes, to taste

Heat the olive oil in a saucepan over a medium heat, add the carrot and celery and sauté for 2–3 minutes until soft. Add the spices and lentils and cook for a further 1–2 minutes until the lentils start to stick to the bottom, then pour over the stock or water and bring to the boil. Stir in the tomatoes and vinegar, reduce the heat and simmer for 20 minutes, until the lentils are cooked through and the soup has thickened and reduced slightly.

Taste and adjust the seasoning to your liking, then ladle into bowls and serve with buttered toast.

Sweet corn fritters

MAKES 10

MRS I love a recipe where you can just throw everything in a bowl and mix it together like this one. These are kid-friendly, work well in the lunchbox and can be transported for a picnic with smashed avo. They are great at breakfast too with a poached free-range egg and relish.

1½ corn cobs, kernels removed

2 spring onions (scallions), finely chopped

½ teaspoon sumac

½ teaspoon ground coriander

½ teaspoon salt flakes

100 g (3½ oz / ⅔ cup) plain (all-purpose) flour

½ teaspoon baking powder

1 free-range egg, beaten

100 ml (3½ fl oz) milk (or nut milk)

3–4 tablespoons extra-virgin olive oil

Put the sweet corn kernels in a bowl together with the spring onions, sumac, coriander, salt, flour and baking powder and mix well. Stir in the egg to combine and pour in the milk, stirring, to form a batter.

Heat 1 tablespoon of olive oil in a frying pan over a medium heat. In batches and using 1 tablespoon of the batter for each fritter, add the batter to the pan and cook for 2–3 minutes on each side until golden and cooked through, adding an extra tablespoon of oil to the pan in between each batch. Eat straightaway with poached eggs, smashed avo and Mr Wilkinson's red sauce (see page 240), or with left-over roasted veggies and a squeeze of lemon juice.

XO prawn omelette

SERVES 2

> **MR** I'm sure that once you've tasted this omelette it will become a firm household favourite. I love XO sauce and vividly remember the first time we made our own at Pope Joan. It was a eureka moment – I couldn't believe that such a great, complex-tasting sauce could be so simple to make. If you don't have time to make it or you can't find it, this will be just as good with black bean sauce or chilli sauce instead.

6 free-range eggs

1 tablespoon soy sauce

1 tablespoon Shaoxing rice wine

¼ teaspoon pepper

100 ml (3½ fl oz) thick cream (double/heavy)

3 tablespoons non-GMO vegetable oil

200 g (7 oz) raw prawns (shrimp), peeled and deveined

3 tablespoons XO sauce (page 243), plus extra to serve

3 spring onions (scallions), chopped

6 coriander (cilantro) sprigs, leaves stripped and stems roughly chopped, plus extra to serve

In a bowl, whisk together the eggs, soy, Shaoxing wine and pepper, then add the thick cream and whisk again.

Heat 1½ tablespoons of the oil in a large frying pan over a medium heat. Add half the prawns and 1½ tablespoons of the XO and stir-fry until the prawns are just cooked, then pour over half the egg mixture. Stir gently until the egg mixture starts to cook, then reduce the heat to low and cook until the omelette has just set. Scatter over half the spring onion and coriander, fold over the omelette and slide onto a serving plate, then repeat for the second omelette.

To serve, spoon a little more XO over the omelettes and garnish with a few extra sprigs of coriander.

Chicken, pineapple & bacon skewers

MAKES 8

> **MRS** Food on sticks is always a winner for the boys. This particular combination was made up by Finn and is a perfect combination of sweet and salty.

500 g (1 lb 2 oz) free-range boneless, skinless chicken thighs, cut into 32 equal-sized pieces

zest and juice of ½ lemon

1 rosemary sprig, leaves removed

pinch of salt flakes

2 tablespoons extra-virgin olive oil

½ pineapple, peeled and cut into 24 equal-sized pieces

8 free-range bacon rashers, cut into 24 equal-sized strips

The Mrs' toasted couscous salad, to serve (page 241)

Soak 8 bamboo skewers in water for 5 minutes.

Put the chicken, lemon zest and juice, rosemary leaves, salt and olive oil in a bowl and mix together well. Leave to marinate for 10 minutes.

Thread the chicken, pineapple and bacon pieces onto the skewers, alternating between the ingredients starting and finishing with a chicken piece. Transfer the skewers to a hot barbecue or chargrill pan and cook over a medium heat for 8–10 minutes, turning every minute or so, until cooked through. Serve with The Mrs' toasted couscous salad (see page 241).

Pumpkin & haloumi tarts

MAKES 4

MR A quintessential menu item at Pope Joan, the idea came from my head chef at the time and friend Jason Newton in 2012 after we did an event where the dessert was an American-style sweet pumpkin tart with liquorice ice cream. A friend of Jason's and his partner, Rhani, was doing an internship for a law firm in New Orleans acting as a defendant for people on death row and the original recipe came from one of the defendant's mothers. It was so sickly sweet but after a little tinkering to make it savoury, here is the result.

1 frozen butter puff pastry sheet, thawed and cut into 4 equal-sized squares

3 tablespoons extra-virgin olive oil

300 g (10½ oz) jap or kent pumpkin (squash) or butternut squash flesh, diced

1 onion, diced

½ teaspoon ras el hanout

50 g (1¾ oz) salted butter

2 free-range eggs, plus 1 extra if needed (see Tip)

100 ml (3½ fl oz) cream

2 tablespoons full-fat milk powder (optional)

80 g (2¾ oz) haloumi, finely diced

dressed salad leaves or fried free-range eggs, to serve (optional)

The Mrs' toasted couscous salad, to serve (optional)

Preheat the oven to 180°C (350°F/Gas 4).

Use the puff pastry squares to line four individual 12 cm (4¾ in) pie tins, rolling the pastry out to make sure the edges hit the rims of the tins if necessary. Fork the pastry at the bottom, then line each pie case with baking paper and cover with baking beads or rice. Bake blind for 8–10 minutes, remove the beads and paper and bake again for 2–4 minutes, or until the pastry is dry to the touch. Remove from the oven and set aside to cool.

Heat the oil in a heavy-based saucepan over a medium–low heat. Add the pumpkin, onion, ras el hanout and butter, cover with a lid and cook for 15 minutes, then remove the lid and cook for a further 10 minutes until the pumpkin is soft.

Tip the cooked pumpkin mixture into a food processor, add the eggs, cream and milk powder, if using, and blitz until smooth. Press the mixture through a sieve to remove any lumps, then spoon it evenly into the four tart cases. Divide the haloumi chunks between the tarts, return to the oven and bake for a further 18–20 minutes, until the filling is set and the top is golden.

Serve the tarts on their own, with a little green salad or the Mrs' toasted couscous salad (page 241), or topped with a fried egg.

TIP *The milk powder here is optional but it definitely gives the filling a creamier texture, so add another egg to the mix if you choose to leave it out.*

Snacks

M R　We have all heard it before, that little voice that tells us to 'just eat a little something, you're hungry'. That voice is called Snack and he's a naughty little bugger. And if you listen to him, before you know it you've opened the fridge or cupboard and ... well, you know the rest.

Snacking is not a new thing (think nuts and dried fruit) and it's actually an essential part of our daily food intake. What is new, however, is that there are now so many processed foods out there that are so conveniently accessible, all packaged up and designed to bombard our taste buds so that we start to crave them – you know the ones: chips (or crisps if you're English), chocolate bars, muesli bars and the like.

We made a conscious decision a while ago to avoid processed foods where possible, working on the logic that if we can make it ourselves, then we don't need to buy it. Now, there are a few exceptions to this rule such as tinned baked beans (not to mention my love of Happy Cow, you know that crazy spreadable cheese in the aluminium foil triangle) or Sharlee's love of Jatz crackers and store-bought hot cross buns, but by and large it works, and nowhere is this truer than for snacks. The following recipes are the things we turn to when we hear those whispers in our heads – here's hoping you find them as useful as we do.

Popcorn

SERVES 2

> **MRS** This is the best bowl snack ever! We serve it plain but you could sprinkle it with salt (or even Herb salt, see page 237) if you like.

Heat 1 tablespoon extra-virgin olive oil in a large saucepan over a medium–low heat. Add a couple of popcorn kernels to the pan and give it a shake. When the kernels pop, remove the pan from the heat, then add another 40 g (1½ oz) kernels in an even layer. Cover the pan with a lid and leave off the heat for 30–40 seconds, then return to the heat, gently shake the pan and wait for the kernels to start popping. Leave on the heat with the lid slightly ajar until the popping slows down. Transfer to a bowl and enjoy.

Hummus & crackers

SERVES 4

> **MR** I love hummus (or 'um-oss', as I pronounce it with my sexy Yorkshire accent) and can't get enough of the stuff. While you can of course use dried chickpeas and soak them overnight, it's a bit of a faff and given that there are some very good tinned ones out there, we don't bother.

Heat 100 ml (3½ fl oz) extra-virgin olive oil in a saucepan over a low heat, add 4 crushed garlic cloves and 400 g (14 oz) drained tinned chickpeas and cook for 2–3 minutes until soft. Leave to cool slightly, then transfer to the blender with 1 tablespoon tahini, the juice of 1 lemon juice and a pinch of salt flakes and blend everything together until smooth. Spoon into a bowl, sprinkle over a pinch each of sumac and paprika and serve with crackers.

Sweet potato wedges & sour cream

SERVES 4

> **MRS** This adult snack always gets gobbled up by the kids.

Preheat the oven to 220°C (430°F/Gas 7) and line a baking tray with paper. Cut 2 sweet potatoes into thick wedges and arrange these on a baking tray in a single layer. Brush all over with 2 tablespoons extra-virgin olive oil and sprinkle over a pinch each of salt flakes, ground fennel and ground coriander. Bake for 20–25 minutes until crisp on the outside and soft in the middle, then pile into a bowl. Serve with a small bowl filled with 60 g (2 oz) sour cream for dipping.

Smashed cannellini beans & veggie sticks

SERVES 4

> **MRS** We love this creamy, tangy purée, which is pretty versatile. It makes a great snack with veggie sticks like this but is also lovely spread on toast, or even served as an accompaniment to grilled fish for dinner.

Heat 2 tablespoons extra-virgin olive oil in a saucepan over a medium heat, add 1 thinly sliced garlic clove and a rosemary sprig and sauté for 1 minute. Add 400 g (14 oz) drained tinned cannellini (lima) beans and stir to coat in the oil, then cook, stirring with a wooden spoon and crushing the beans gently against the sides of the pan, for 6–8 minutes until broken down to a rough purée, adding a little boiling water as you go if it looks in danger of drying out. Add a pinch of salt and the juice of 1 lemon and mix together well, adding a little more boiling water if necessary to loosen things up. Spoon the smashed beans into a bowl and serve with e carrot, cucumber and celery sticks.

Grape lightsabres

MAKES AS MANY AS YOU WANT

MRS This is part-snack, part-craft activity. I found it while searching for Star Wars party ideas and I'm glad I did, as these were by far the most popular snack on the party table.

Wrap some wine bottle corks tightly with aluminium foil. Cut small squares and rectangles out of some coloured tape with a pair of scissors and stick these onto the corks – these will be the buttons for your lightsabre handles. Thread grapes (red or white depending on which side of the force is strongest with you) lengthways onto the skewers, leaving 5 cm (2 in) clear at the pointed ends, then push the pointed ends into the cork 'handles' to complete. Keep refrigerated until ready to eat.

Chocolate almonds

MAKES APPROX. 130 G (4½ OZ)

MRS Two of our favourite things packed up into one snack.

Set a stainless steel bowl over a saucepan filled with 3 cm (1¼ in) water. Bring the water to a simmer, add 90 g (3 oz) dark chocolate broken into small pieces and melt slowly, stirring to break up any lumps. Remove the bowl from the pan and place on a work surface. Cover a baking tray with baking paper. Tip 80 g (2¾ oz/½ cup) almonds into the melted chocolate and stir together well, then pour the melted chocolate and almond mixture onto the baking paper and spread it out to cover the sheet evenly. Sprinkle over a good pinch of salt flakes, then transfer to the fridge to set. Once set, break into bite-size pieces and store in an airtight container in the fridge until needed.

Cheese 'n' Jatz

MAKES 16

> **MRS** This was a family fave growing up and would make an appearance around 5 pm on a weekend arvo. For me, Jatz can never be replaced by the Savoy alternative that is so readily found here in Victoria, though you can of course sub in your own favourite cracker. These are perfect for taking into the garden on a lazy afternoon (and Matt would say, best served with a cold beer).

Layer up a Jatz cracker or other savoury cracker with a similar-sized slice of cheddar and a slice of sweet spiced gherkin (pickle). Eat straight away, then repeat as you like.

Soft-boiled egg & soldiers

SERVES 1

> **MR** Many a word has been written about how to boil an egg, but it still surprises me how many home or professional cooks in this crazy, food-obsessed age don't know how to boil (or poach) one properly. Here's my advice. Just mind you don't burn the toast, and if your soldiers are bigger than an egg, well, you're a fool.

Fill a saucepan with water three-quarters full and bring to the boil. Lower a medium free-range egg straight from the fridge gently onto the bottom of the pan using a slotted spoon and boil for 5 minutes. Remove with the slotted spoon and set onto a plate to dry for 1 minute, then transfer to your favourite egg cup (we all have one). Serve with a slice of toast buttered right to the crust and cut into soldiers. Enjoy.

Banana whip

SERVES 2

MRS This is so, so simple, but so tasty and (if your household is anything like ours) will be sure to become a firm favourite. It's great served simply like this or dressed up with a scattering of chopped roasted nuts and a drizzle of salted caramel sauce. Just make sure you peel the bananas before you freeze them – trying to peel a frozen banana is a nightmare.

Throw 2 frozen bananas into a food processor and blitz to a soft whipped texture. Divide between bowls and serve.

Strawberry & coconut icy poles

MAKES 6

MRS These are always on standby in the freezer for a hot day. We have an awesome collection of icy-pole moulds and tubes in the cupboard but you can really use any small plastic container to freeze the mix, just add an icy-pole stick (I've even used wooden teaspoons for the stick before). The strawberries can be swapped out for pretty much any soft fruit you have to hand – blueberries, mango or pineapple all work well – just keep the quantities to two parts fruit and one part coconut cream and you'll be fine.

Wash 250 g (9 oz) hulled strawberries really well and pat dry with paper towel, then place in a blender with 125 ml (4 fl oz/½ cup) coconut cream and 2 teaspoons honey. Blitz together on a high speed to a smooth purée, then pour into six 70 ml (2¼ fl oz) capacity icy-pole moulds, popping an icy-pole stick into each. Leave to freeze overnight.

Green ice pops

MAKES 4

MRS Being icy poles, no-one minds that these are green, making them one of the easiest ways I know of getting a few leafy veggies into growing bodies. As Finn would say, 'I love icy poles because they are cold and delicious'. Magic!

Add the flesh of 1 mango, 1 banana, 4 kale leaves and 250 ml (8½ fl oz/1 cup) apple juice to a food processor or blender and blitz to a smooth purée. Pour into four 70 ml (2¼ fl oz) capacity icy-pole moulds, popping an icy-pole stick into each. Freeze overnight.

Pineapple pops

MAKES 4

MRS This is one of my favourite juice combos. Pineapple gets a lovely creaminess to it when it goes through the juicer and this works really well in an icy pole.

Cut 2 green apples and the flesh of ½ pineapple into rough chunks. Before turning on the juicer, pop a handful of mint leaves into the chute followed by a quarter of the apple (this will help push the mint leaves through). Juice into a jug (pitcher), feeding in the pineapple and remaining apple. Stir the juice gently and pour into four 70 ml (2¼ fl oz) capacity icy-pole moulds. Pop an icy-pole stick into each mould and freeze overnight.

Sunday Baking Sessions

M R I'm lying in bed with my eyes closed and that unmistakable smell wafts through the room – the one that throws me straight back to being a child and bursting into the kitchens of my aunties Mary and Betty or my Nanna. She's at it again. It's Sunday and Sharlee is in her pinny and baking. BOOM!

Is it a cake? Is it those jam drop biscuits? Is it that upside-down tart she promised me while we were courting (and which took her two blinking years to make) or is it those chewy chocolate and fennel cookies that the whole family goes nuts for? Whatever it might be, the three of us follow that delicious aroma like rats following the Pied Piper. This is a memory in the making, a food moment that we all love.

The Mrs likes to change things up a little from time to time with her sweet treats – whether that's through the use of alternative sweeteners or by changing a flour to keep us on our toes – and the following recipes are a collection of our home favourites together with a couple of all-time classics from Pope Joan. 'But Matt, do you bake?', I hear you ask ... Well, let's just say I look great in that pinny too and leave it at that.

Edna's biscuits

MAKES 20

MRS My nana Edna used to make these biscuits for me when I was little. She always had a few tins of biscuits to offer when I would go to stay with her for the school holidays, but these were my favourite. We would munch on them while playing canasta and reading *Woman's Day* cut-out recipes. Originally they were called tandem biscuits, as the fork prints on them look like the old school tandem ploughs used on farms, but we changed the name in memory of Edna.

55 g (2 oz/1 cup) coconut flakes

125 g (4½ oz/ ½ cup) butter, at room temperature

165 g (6 oz/ ¾ cup) raw (demerara) sugar

1 free-range egg, beaten

225 g (8 oz/1½ cups) self-raising flour

3 heaped teaspoons custard powder

Preheat the oven to 160°C (320°F/Gas 3). Line two baking trays with baking paper.

Put the coconut flakes in a food processor and blitz to fine breadcrumb-like pieces. Set aside.

Beat the butter and sugar together in a bowl with an electric mixer until light and fluffy. Add the egg and whisk until combined, then add self-raising flour and custard powder to form a dough.

Scoop out teaspoonfuls of the dough and roll into small balls. Arrange the balls on the prepared baking trays leaving 2 cm (¾ in) or so between each to allow for spreading when baking, then press down on the dough with a fork to flatten the biscuits.

Bake for 15 minutes until lightly golden (keeping an eye on them to make sure they don't burn). Remove from the oven, cool on a wire rack and store in an airtight container for up to 5 days.

Pictured on page 90

Chocolate & fennel cookies

MAKES 20 LARGE COOKIES OR HEAPS OF LITTLE ONES

> **MRS** These are our favourite cookies. One day, wanting to make a gluten-free chocolate cookie, I came across some dark chocolate laced with fennel seeds in the pantry so I experimented, and the results got the thumbs up from everyone. The secret with these is to take the cookies from the oven when they are just slightly soft to give you a lovely, chewy texture. I have used coconut sugar instead of raw sugar here before with the same results, just be aware that coconut sugar darkens more quickly when cooking. If you don't have coconut flour in the cupboard you could always use plain flour instead.

50 g (1¾ oz) unsalted butter, diced

160 g (5½ oz) dark chocolate, roughly chopped

2 free-range eggs

220 g (8 oz/1 cup) coconut sugar (or raw (demerara) sugar)

1 teaspoon vanilla paste

30 g (1 oz) coconut flour (or plain flour if not making gluten-free)

1 teaspoon fennel seeds

65 g (2¼ oz) raw almonds, roughly chopped (optional)

½ teaspoon baking powder (we use gluten-free baking powder)

pinch of salt flakes

Preheat the oven to 180°C (350°F/Gas 4). Line two baking trays with baking paper.

Melt the butter and chocolate together in a saucepan over a low heat. Set aside to cool.

Put the eggs, sugar and vanilla in a bowl and whisk together with an electric beater for 2–3 minutes until nice and thick. Stir in the melted chocolate with a wooden spoon to combine, then add the coconut flour, fennel seeds, almonds, baking powder and salt. Stir together to form a wet dough, then leave to sit for a few minutes (this will allow the coconut flour to absorb more of the liquid, making the dough easier to handle).

Using a dessert spoon (or a teaspoon if you like your cookies small), drop spoonfuls of the dough onto the baking tray in rough circles, leaving 2 cm (¾ in) or so between each to allow the cookies to spread when baking.

Bake for 10–12 minutes until set but still soft, then remove from the tray carefully with a spatula and transfer to a wire rack to cool. Keep in an airtight container for up to 5 days.

Pictured on page 91

Plum jam drops

MAKES APPROX. 24

> **MRS** These are the first biscuits that Finn and I started making together. You can use any jam you have in the cupboard here (especially the one lurking at the back you bought at the school fête) or try this quick, no-cook option instead – any leftovers you have can be kept in a sealed jar in the fridge for up 5 days and are good for breakfast.

115 g (4 oz) unsalted butter, at room temperature

130 g (4½ oz) sugar

1 free-range egg

1 teaspoon vanilla paste

200 g (7 oz/1⅓ cups) plain (all-purpose) flour

½ teaspoon baking powder

150 g (5½ oz) plum jam (see below), or 150 g (5½ oz) pre-made jam of your choice

PLUM JAM

300 g (10½ oz) plums, stones removed

1 tablespoon maple syrup

1 teaspoon vanilla paste

juice of ½ lemon

2 tablespoons chia seeds

To make the jam, put the plums, maple syrup, vanilla paste and lemon juice in a food processor and blitz until smooth, scraping down the sides with a spatula as you go to ensure that no large pieces of fruit are left. Stir in the chia seeds and mix together well, then pour into a clean jar and transfer to the fridge for 30 minutes to chill and thicken to a jam-like consistency.

Preheat the oven to 180°C (350°F/Gas 4). Line two baking trays with baking paper.

In a bowl, cream the butter and sugar together with an electric whisk until light and fluffy. Add the egg and vanilla paste and whisk to combine, then gently stir in the flour and baking powder with a wooden spoon to form a dough.

Scoop out teaspoonfuls of the dough and roll into small balls. Arrange the balls on the prepared baking trays leaving 2 cm (¾ in) or so between each to allow for spreading when baking, then press down on the centre of each ball with your thumb to make holes.

Spoon ¾ teaspoon of jam into each of the holes, being careful not to overfill them as the jam will run over while baking, and bake for 10–12 minutes on the top shelf of the oven until golden. Leave to cool on a wire rack. Keep stored in an airtight container for up to 4–5 days.

Anzac biscuit ice cream sandwiches

MAKES 16 BISCUITS OR 8 SANDWICHES

MRS While everyone loves an Anzac bickie, adding in your favourite ice cream takes them to the next level. These ice cream sandwiches are perfect for parties – make the biscuits up in advance and take the ice cream out of the freezer to soften just before serving and then it's just a case of scooping and sandwiching together. Be warned though, things can get messy!

100 g (3½ oz/1 cup) rolled (porridge) oats

40 g (1½ oz/ ¾ cup) toasted coconut flakes

150 g (5½ oz/1 cup) plain (all-purpose) flour

pinch of salt flakes

110 g (4 oz/ ½ cup) raw (demerara) sugar

120 g (4½ oz) unsalted butter

2 tablespoons golden syrup

1 teaspoon bicarbonate of soda (baking soda)

tub of your favourite ice cream, to serve

Preheat the oven to 180°C (350°F/Gas 4). Line two baking trays with baking paper.

Mix together the oats, coconut flakes, flour, salt and sugar in a large bowl.

Melt together the butter and syrup in a saucepan over a low heat. Remove from the heat, stir in 2 tablespoons hot water, bicarbonate of soda and oat mixture and mix well to combine.

Take teaspoonfuls of the mixture and roll into even-shaped balls, then arrange on the prepared baking trays, leaving 2 cm (¾ in) or so between each to allow for spreading when baking. Flatten the balls slightly using a wooden spoon or the palm of your hand, then bake for 15 minutes, or until golden but still a little soft. Leave to cool on a wire rack.

To serve, place a scoop of your favourite ice cream between two of the biscuits and sandwich together. Enjoy!

Chocolate brownies

MAKES 12

> **MR** A Pope Joan classic, we have had these in the cake cabinet since the day we opened and I have to say they're really good. We serve them with whipped cream or vanilla ice cream – pure gold.

100 g (3½ oz) dark chocolate

100 g (3½ oz) unsalted butter

100 g (3½ oz) brown sugar

2 free-range eggs, beaten

1 teaspoon vanilla paste

65 g (2¼ oz/ ⅔ cup) ground almonds

1 teaspoon cocoa powder

whipped cream or vanilla ice cream, to serve

Preheat the oven to 180°C (350°F/Gas 4). Grease and line a 20 x 20 cm (8 x 8 in) baking tin with baking paper.

Melt the chocolate, butter and sugar together in a large bowl over a saucepan of lightly simmering water. Once melted, remove the bowl from the heat, stir everything together again and leave to cool slightly. Whisk in the eggs, then add the remaining ingredients and stir to combine.

Pour the batter into the baking tin and bake for 20–25 minutes, until cracked and dry on top. Remove from the oven and leave to cool in the tin before cutting into 12 squares. Serve with whipped cream or vanilla ice cream.

TIP *The brownies will keep in a suitable airtight container in the fridge for up to 7 days and are best warmed in an oven preheated to 180°C (350°F/Gas 4) for 4 minutes before serving.*

Nonna Leah's boiled fruit cake

MAKES 1 CAKE

MRS Loaded with dried fruit, which gives it a lovely colour and helps to keep it nice and moist, this cake is the bomb. My Mum has been baking this fruit cake at Christmas for as long as I can remember – in fact, when I was living overseas I insisted she send me the recipe so I could make it for Christmas myself. She duly did, faxing the page over to me (this was 2001) straight from her original recipe book, complete with measurements in pounds and ounces and handwritten notes and corrections.

60 g (2 oz/¼ cup) unsalted butter

250 ml (8½ fl oz/1 cup) milk

110 g (4 oz/ ½ cup) raw (demerara) sugar

500 g (1 lb 2 oz) mixed dried fruit (my Mum uses mixed peel, glacé cherries, sultanas (golden raisins) and dates)

50 g (1¾ oz) walnuts, chopped

½ teaspoon ground nutmeg

1 teaspoon mixed spice

250 ml (8½ fl oz/1 cup) dry sherry

¾ teaspoon bicarbonate of soda (baking soda)

2 free-range eggs, beaten

300 g (10½ oz/2 cups) plain wholemeal (whole-wheat) flour or plain (all-purpose) flour

2 teaspoons baking powder

1 handful whole almonds

Preheat the oven to 180°C (350°F/Gas 4). Grease and line a 22 cm (8¾ in) round cake tin with baking paper.

Add the butter, milk, sugar, dried fruit, walnuts and spices to a saucepan over a medium heat. Bring to the boil, stirring gently with a wooden spoon to dissolve the sugar as you go, then lower the heat and let simmer for 5 minutes. Remove from the heat and leave to cool, then add the sherry, bicarbonate of soda and beaten eggs and mix well. Fold in the flour and baking powder to form a batter.

Pour the batter into the prepared cake tin, arrange the almonds over the top and bake for 60 minutes, or until a skewer inserted into the centre comes out clean. Leave to cool slightly in the tin, then turn out onto a wire rack to cool completely. Keep in an airtight container for up to 7 days.

Pictured on page 101

Lemon, polenta & almond cake

MAKES 1 CAKE

> **MRS** This is a fab cake which holds together well for the lunchbox but can also be prettied up for a dessert. To make it gluten-free, simply replace the regular baking powder with the gluten-free variety.

100 g (3½ oz/⅔ cup) polenta

zest and juice of 1 lemon

200 g (7 oz) unsalted butter, at room temperature

120 g (4½ oz/ ½ cup) raw (demerara) sugar

1 tablespoon honey

1 teaspoon vanilla paste

3 free-range eggs

150 g (5½ oz) ground almonds

1 teaspoon baking powder

pinch of salt flakes

Add the polenta to a small bowl with the lemon juice and 3 tablespoons warm water, mix together and leave to soak for 30 minutes.

Preheat the oven to 180°C (350°F/Gas 4). Grease and line a 20 cm (8 in) round cake tin.

In a separate bowl, beat the butter, sugar and honey together until creamy. Add the vanilla paste and lemon zest and mix together well, then add the eggs one at a time, beating well between each, until well combined. Stir in the ground almonds, baking powder, salt and polenta mixture and mix well to form a batter.

Pour the batter into the prepared cake tin and bake for 50 minutes, or until golden brown on top and a skewer inserted into the centre comes out clean. (The cake will brown quickly, so keep an eye that it doesn't burn and cover it with foil if needed.) Remove from the oven and leave to cool in the cake tin, then slice and serve with yoghurt and berries or keep it in an airtight container for up to 5 days for adding to lunchboxes.

Pictured on page 101

Yorkshire custard tarts

MAKES 8

MR Ok, ok, I'm pretty crap at baking – bread dough looks at me and flops, scones in my hands transform into rocks while, for some inexplicable reason, I've even been known to mistake salt for sugar. These custard tarts, though, I can make (on a good day – they are from Yorkshire after all) and they taste so good that they almost make up for my spectacular lack of baking talent. Almost.

1 free-range egg plus 2 free-range egg yolks

100 g (3½ oz) raw (demerara) sugar

1½ tablespoons cornflour (cornstarch)

310 ml (10½ fl oz/1¼ cups) milk

125 ml (4 fl oz/ ½ cup) thick (double/heavy) cream

¼ teaspoon vanilla paste

2 frozen butter puff pastry sheets, thawed

60 g (2 oz/ ½ cup) icing (confectioner's) sugar

½ teaspoon ground cinnamon

¼ teaspoon ground cloves

Grease eight 10 x 2.5 cm (4 x 1 in) deep flan (tart) tins with a little butter.

In a bowl, whisk together the egg, egg yolks, raw sugar and cornflour until pale and creamy.

Add the milk, cream and vanilla paste to a saucepan and bring to a simmer, then remove from the heat, pour in the egg mixture and whisk together well to combine. Return the mixture to the pan (using a spatula to get the last little bits out of the bowl), place it back on the heat and cook, stirring, over a low heat until thickened to a pasty glue-like consistency. Spoon the custard into a bowl and cover with plastic wrap, then transfer to the fridge and leave to cool.

On a floured work surface, cut the pastry out into 15 cm (6 in) circles and prick them all over with a fork. Carefully lay the pastry into the tins, pressing it into the edges.

Combine the icing sugar, cinnamon and clove in a bowl, then transfer it to a sieve. Sift half the icing sugar mixture over the pastry cases, then place the tins in the fridge and leave to rest for 5 minutes.

Preheat the oven to 180°C (350°F/Gas 4).

Spoon the custard filling into the pastry cases, dust with the remaining icing sugar mixture and bake for 18–22 minutes until the custard is set and the tops are golden and caramelised. Remove from the oven and leave to sit in the tins for 5 minutes before transferring to a wire rack to cool.

Peach tartlets

MAKES 4

> **MRS** I made these as an impromptu dessert one night on the fly and they were magic. You could use other stone fruit like nectarines here or even a big handful of cherries instead.

2 large ready-to-eat peaches, quartered, or 4 small peaches, halved and stones removed

2 tablespoons honey

8 small thyme sprigs

1 frozen butter puff pastry sheet, thawed

vanilla ice cream or whipped cream, to serve

Preheat the oven to 180°C (350°F/Gas 4). Line a baking tray with baking paper.

Put the peach pieces skin side down in a saucepan with the honey, half the thyme and 2–3 tablespoons boiling water and cook over a low heat, with the lid on, until slightly softened, about 5–6 minutes.

Cut the puff pastry sheet into quarters and lay them out on the prepared baking tray. On each of the pastry squares gently score a line about 1 cm (½ in) in from the edges using a small sharp knife.

Lay two peach pieces skin side down in the centre of one of the puff pastry squares and drizzle over a little of the syrup from the pan, then fold over the edges of the pastry to the scored line to form a raised border (this will stop the honey from spreading during cooking). Repeat with the remaining peach pieces and puff pastry squares and top each with a thyme sprig.

Transfer to the oven and bake for 30 minutes, or until the pastry is golden brown. Serve warm with a dollop of vanilla ice cream or softly whipped cream.

Strawberry frangipane tart

SERVES 4

> **MRS** This is a cheat's frangipane tart as it's served in the dish, meaning there's no base to worry about. The strawberries here can be subbed out for whatever seasonal fresh fruit you have to hand – figs would work well, as would cherries or soft stone fruit.

80 g (2¾ oz) unsalted butter, at room temperature

80 g (2¾ oz) raw (demerara) sugar

1 teaspoon vanilla paste

1 free-range egg

100 g (3½ oz/1 cup) ground almonds

1 tablespoon cornflour (cornstarch)

8 strawberries, hulled and halved

vanilla ice cream, to serve

Preheat the oven to 180°C (350°F/Gas 4). Grease a 16 cm (6¼ in) round ovenproof dish with a little butter.

Using an electric mixer, beat the butter and sugar together in a bowl until light and fluffy. Add the vanilla and egg and whisk until combined, then stir in the ground almonds and cornflour to form a batter.

Pour the batter into the dish and arrange the strawberries on top in concentric circles. Bake for 40 minutes or until golden brown on top and a skewer inserted into the centre comes out clean. (If the top starts to brown too quickly cover it with foil while cooking.)

Leave to cool slightly, then transfer the dish to the table and serve warm with vanilla ice cream.

A NOTE ON VANILLA FROM MATT ...

Vanilla is the only fruit-bearing plant of the orchid family. It has to be hand-pollinated when the flower blooms to produce the bean, which spends nine months on the plant before being picked green and then undergoes a series of drying and curing processes to produce the vanilla bean we all know. Most vanilla flavourings you see in the market aren't actually real vanilla; instead they are made from vanillin – a cheap, synthetic flavouring derived from by-products that imitate the flavour of vanilla, so please check the label and don't use it. The true flavour for me is such an exotic, beautiful taste that goes brilliantly with both sweet and savoury dishes.

The best way to ensure you are buying real vanilla is to buy a fresh pod, but this can come with a hefty price tag and a lack of freshness as the pods can dry out a little. The alternative is to buy a paste or extract (though be sure to check the label to make sure that there is only real vanilla in it). The vanilla paste I use is made by a wonderful family-run company called Heilala Vanilla, which was started as an aid project in 2002 by the Ross family and villagers on the island of Vavu'a in the Kingdom of Tonga and now helps other growers in Tonga farm ethically produced, sustainable vanilla, together with new partnerships in Uganda and the Cook Islands.

Picnics

MR I do believe that along with the good old barbecue, Sir Donald Bradman and the mullet haircut, another thing that is quite truly Australian is the picnic. Think about the vast space we have in this country – from the stunning national parks, beaches, rainforests and deserts to the amazing little townships dotted around with their cute little gardens and memorial areas, this is one big picnic land. And when the weather's fine what better way is there to enjoy a wonderful day out than gathered somewhere with family and friends with the cricket bats and a footy, a musical instrument or the wireless, and a blanket and picnic basket in tow?

We as a family have enjoyed many an excellent picnic in this beautiful land of ours, as well as in many other countries across the world. And a good picnic doesn't take much more than access to good, simple food – think baguettes, a good local brie with a few pickles, some sliced salami, a little frittata, hummus, crackers and raw veg sticks, then throw in a portable barbecue for sausages and you've already hit upon pure picnicking gold. Add a cheeky pavlova or lemon polenta cake to finish along with some homemade cordial and sparkling water to drink and you've hit the jackpot (and that's before I've even suggested packing that bottle of wine in the esky).

This chapter is full of the things we love to eat on a picnic – delicious, easy to prepare, transportable dishes that adults and kids alike love. Don't think your picnics should be limited to this selection alone though, as there are lots of other recipes throughout the rest of the book that can also be enjoyed in the great outdoors. Just remember, if you can pack it, you can picnic on it.

Pea, mint & ricotta filo tartlets

MAKES 6

> **MRS** These gorgeous little tarts are what spring tastes like to me. They are so easy to make and the filling ingredients can be easily substituted for whatever is in season.

1½ tablespoons extra-virgin olive oil, for brushing

2 filo pastry sheets

80 g (2¾ oz/ ½ cup) peas, fresh or frozen

125 g (4½ oz/ ½ cup) ricotta

zest of ½ lemon

1 handful mint leaves, finely chopped

4 free-range eggs

pinch of salt flakes

Preheat the oven to 180°C (350°F/Gas 4). Brush a 6-hole muffin tin with olive oil.

Lay one of the filo sheets onto a clean work surface and brush lightly with olive oil. Cut the sheet in half lengthways and then into thirds widthways to leave you with 6 rough squares. Line the muffin tin with the squares, pushing them down fully into each holes, then repeat the process with the second filo sheet, this time placing the squares on a different angle to create star-shaped tartlet cases.

Mix the remaining ingredients together in a bowl until well combined. Spoon the filling evenly into the tartlet cases and bake for 20 minutes or until the filling is cooked through.

A NOTE ON OLIVE OIL FROM MATT ...
Here in Australia we make some of the best olive oil in the world. All Australian-produced olive oil is classed as extra-virgin olive oil and is made naturally without synthetics, which cannot be said for many of the substandard imported olive oils seen on the market. Where we use a different oil in a recipe (usually using a GM-free vegetable oil instead) it's normally a question of taste, as we don't want that beautiful flavour of olive oil to become part of the dish.

I'll be honest, I didn't always like olive oil. I'm a butter and lard kind of guy and it took me a few years to get used to its herbaceous, peppery tones. It was visiting the groves of Cobram Estate that really changed my mind and developed my appreciation for it – they have over 2.4 million trees across the Murray River valley with 14 different varieties of olives, and they crush and cold-press these olives within 4–6 hours of harvest to ensure freshness and maximum flavour. There are hundreds of other brilliant olive oil producers in Australia and buying local not only supports them but also gets you the best product possible as, like fresh herbs, olive oil needs to be at its freshest to be at its best.

Pictured on page 114

Zucchini bread, salami, cheese & pickles

SERVES 4

> **MR** This makes for something a little different to take to a picnic, though saying that I could just as easily devour it for supper with a good bottle of chardonnay. Delicious.

300 ml (10 fl oz) white-wine vinegar

300 g (10½ oz) sugar

pinch of saffron threads

pinch of chilli flakes

1 fennel bulb, halved and thinly sliced

1 salad onion or white onion, halved and thinly sliced

1 carrot, thinly sliced

200 g (7 oz) soft marinated feta

100 g (3½ oz) sliced salami (or another lovely cured meat such as ham, prosciutto or bresaola)

ZUCCHINI BREAD

350 g (12½ oz) small zucchini (courgettes), coarsely grated

pinch of salt flakes

100 ml (3½ fl oz) extra-virgin olive oil

3 free-range eggs

zest of 1 lemon

300 g (10½ oz/2 cups) self-raising flour

½ teaspoon bicarbonate of soda (baking soda)

2 tablespoons raw (demerara) sugar

pinch of ground cinnamon

pinch of freshly grated nutmeg

Preheat the oven to 180°C (350°F/Gas 4) and lightly grease and flour a 24 x 12 x 6 cm (9½ in x 4¾ in x 2½ in) loaf (bar) tin.

To make the zucchini bread, add the grated zucchini and salt to a bowl. Leave to stand for 10 minutes, then rinse off the salt with cold water and drain. Squeeze out the zucchini over the sink to remove any excess moisture, then transfer to a bowl together with the olive oil, eggs and lemon zest and mix together well.

In a separate bowl, mix together the flour, bicarb, sugar, cinnamon and nutmeg. Fold the dry mixture through the wet mixture until fully incorporated, then pour the batter into the loaf tin and bake for 50–70 minutes, or when a skewer inserted into the centre comes out clean. Remove from the oven and leave to cool slightly in the tin for 10 minutes before turning out.

Add 300 ml (10 fl oz) water, vinegar, sugar, saffron and chilli flakes to a saucepan and bring to the boil. Remove from the heat, pour the hot pickling liquid into a sterilised jar, add the vegetables and leave to cool (at this point they will be ready to serve).

To serve, cut the zucchini bread up into slices and smear them with the feta, then top with the salami and pickles.

Pictured on page 115

Watermelon pizza

SERVES 4

> **MRS** The hooligans were first served this as dessert in a friend's cafe a few years ago and it has been a firm favourite ever since. Don't see the fruits listed here as a fixed list. Use whatever you love – just be sure to make it colourful!

1 × 3 cm (1¼ in) watermelon slice, cut into 6–8 triangular wedges

100 g (3½ oz) blueberries or raspberries

100 g (3½ oz/ ⅔ cup) strawberries, hulled and halved

1 apple, cored, halved and cut into thin slices

1 peach, stone removed and cut into 8 wedges

1 handful mint or chocolate mint leaves

Lay the watermelon pieces out onto a large serving plate to make a rough circle. Top with the rest of the fruit and scatter over the mint leaves to finish. Best served cold.

Pictured on page 114

Smoked salmon, lemon & avo wraps

MAKES 2

> **MRS** Wraps are an essential part of our pantry and this combo works like a dream. We've suggested some other rad fillings below.

100 g (3½ oz) cream cheese

juice of ½ lemon

2 large wholemeal (whole-wheat) wraps

200 g (7 oz) smoked salmon, separated into thin strips

1 Lebanese (short) cucumber, sliced

½ avocado, sliced

Mix the cream cheese and lemon juice together in a bowl until well combined.

Lay the wraps out on a board and spread a thick layer of the cream cheese down the middle of each from top to bottom. Top the cream cheese first with strips of smoked salmon, then slices of cucumber and lastly slices of avocado. Turn the wrap horizontal to the board and roll up tightly to seal.

TIP *While almost anything works inside a wrap, other fillings could include: bacon, omelette, baby spinach and sweet chilli sauce; grilled haloumi, roasted red capsicums (bell peppers) and rocket (arugula); roast chicken, pesto and feta.*

Pictured on page 118

Uncle Deano's 'RG' cobb salad

SERVES 4

MR 'Who is this Uncle Deano?', I hear you say. 'He sounds like trouble.' Well, he is and he's one half of our best friends Nessie and Deano. Deano used to be the private chef on board the late great entrepreneur Reg Grundy's boat and 'RG' used to eat this nearly every day. Deano made this recently for us on holiday together and it rocks.

¼ iceberg lettuce, finely sliced

3 vine-ripened tomatoes, cut into quarters, seeds removed and finely diced

100 g (3½ oz) grated cheddar

6 free-range bacon rashers, thinly sliced and fried till crisp

3 hard-boiled free-range eggs, grated

300 g (10½ oz) cooked skinless free-range chicken breast, diced

1 large handful curly parsley, chopped

100 g (3½ oz) blue cheese, diced

2 tablespoons toasted pine nuts (optional), to serve

150 ml (5 fl oz) Derby dressing (see below)

DERBY DRESSING

90 ml (3 fl oz) worcestershire sauce

3 tablespoons red-wine vinegar

1 teaspoon hot English mustard

zest and juice of 1 lemon

2 garlic cloves, crushed

250 ml (8 ½ fl oz/1 cup) non-GMO vegetable oil

salt flakes

To make the dressing whisk together the worcestershire sauce, vinegar, mustard, lemon juice and zest and crushed garlic in a bowl, then lightly whisk in the oil until combined. Season with salt to taste.

Arrange the iceberg lettuce over a serving platter so that it covers the base evenly, then layer the salad ingredients carefully over the lettuce in individual rows starting with the tomatoes and following with the cheddar, bacon, egg, chicken, parsley and blue cheese to finish (this is all about the presentation, so be careful here). If you're going for the pine nut upgrade, sprinkle them over the top now.

Place the salad in the middle of the table alongside the dressing and let everyone help themselves. Yum.

Pictured on page 119

Orange yoghurt cake

SERVES 6–8

> **MRS** I love that you can use the whole orange in this recipe, it's brilliant. Just make sure you use the unwaxed variety from your neighbour's tree.

1 whole unwaxed orange, skin on, trimmed and roughly cut into chunks

2 free-range eggs

150 g (5½ oz) raw (demerara) sugar

1 teaspoon vanilla paste

240 g (8½ oz) plain (all-purpose) flour

2 teaspoons baking powder

150 g (5½ oz) natural yoghurt, plus extra to serve

100 ml (3½ fl oz) extra-virgin olive oil

Preheat the oven to 180°C (350°F/Gas 4). Grease and line a 22 cm (8¾ in) round cake tin.

Add the orange pieces to a food processor and blitz together to form a smooth paste. Add the eggs, sugar and vanilla and blitz again until light and fluffy, then add the flour and baking powder and pulse to combine. Add the yoghurt and olive oil and pulse again to form a thick, wet batter.

Pour the batter into the cake tin and bake for 50–60 minutes until the top of the cake is lightly golden and a skewer inserted into the centre comes out clean. Leave to cool slightly in the tin for 5–10 minutes, then transfer to a wire rack and leave to cool completely. Slice and serve with a spoonful of natural yoghurt.

Pictured on page 118

Recipes to take on a picnic

Below is a list of other great things we would take on a picnic, cooking at home and taking the cold dishes with us.

All the recipes from the Lunchbox chapter, as well as some from the Snacks and Sunday Baking Sessions chapters are perfect for a picnic. Others that work well are:

DOUBLE CHEESE QUESADILLAS (PAGE 56)

SILVERBEET & FETA TRIANGLES (PAGE 58)

HAWAIIAN PIZZA (PAGE 60)

CHICKEN & MISO NOODLE SALAD (PAGE 62)

CHICKEN, PINEAPPLE & BACON SKEWERS (PAGE 72)

PUMPKIN & HALOUMI TARTS (PAGE 74)

CORNISH SANDWICH (PAGE 142)

BACON & EGG PIE (PAGE 134)

ZUCCHINI SLICE (PAGE 136)

A NOTE ON SEASONALITY FROM MATT ...

We take a seasonal approach to ingredients at Pope Joan, not to try and get media attention by being all hip and different, but because we truly believe in it, which is why we do the same at home and when we are on holiday, too. So what does eating seasonally mean to us? Well, I start by taking the state of Victoria as my country, then I get out my seasonality chart and say to myself that I will eat what grows here when it is in season, and then, if what I want to eat doesn't grow here, I will buy so long as it has been grown in Australia only. It annoys me that a country as large as Australia with such brilliant agriculture and a range of climates that mean produce can be in season for long periods of time should import any fresh fruit or vegetables. I'll say this, local seasonal food tastes so much better. Fact. All the wasted energy it takes to grow and transport food across the globe is simply nuts and is an absolute waste of precious resources, not to mention the fact that those foods will be lacking in flavour. I've said it in my introduction and I will say it again – if you buy well-produced, seasonal tasty ingredients then you are already winning.

Seasonal eating is not always easy, though, and while summer and autumn are simple enough, during winter and into spring when you'd like a juicy, mouthwatering piece of fruit or a vegetable like a cucumber, say, it can become really hard. We ask the kids all the time what they would like to eat and in the depths of winter it's, 'Dad, can I have a peach, or some tomatoes, or corn, or cucumber?'. We discuss this at the table and explain about Dad's crazy beliefs, about what's growing in our garden and on friends' farms. It's tough, so for the last couple of years in winter I ask the clan to name one fruit and one vegetable that is out of season that isn't tomatoes or strawberries that they would like over winter. The answer's always the same – watermelon and cucumbers. And I can't tell you how happy it makes me when in the winter we let the boys know that we are going to Queensland on holiday and I hear Finn shout for joy as he goes 'Dad, that means tomatoes and strawberries are in season and we get to eat them!'

Pies

MRS I reckon we have a pie most weeks; it's a good weeknight option. Some of them require the filling to be cooked on the stove, which I sometimes do in the morning if I wake up early – we are in the kitchen hanging out at breakfast and making lunchboxes anyway. That way I can store the pie in the fridge during the day and pop it in the oven close to dinner time. It greatly reduces my time in the kitchen during the evening, which is great.

Speaking of saving time, one of our freezer essentials is a packet of butter puff pastry sheets. They are so versatile. You can of course go hardcore and make your own puff, but who has time? I put that on the list with peeling sticky labels off bottles and sifting flour – life is too short, right?

Pies are another really good way of getting lots of vegetables into our meals, as well as using up leftovers and surplus eggs. I made my silverbeet and feta pie the other day and put some left-over orzo salad in it as I didn't have many greens to hand. I was unsure how it was going to turn out but the end result was fab as it gave the pie an extra thickness it doesn't usually have. Put that down in the happy accidents pile.

Beef & mushroom pie

SERVES 4

MR This pie is perfect for winter days. I usually cook the filling the day before while getting that night's dinner ready, spooning it into the pie dish and leaving it to cool before transferring it to the fridge. Then the next day it's as simple as popping the pastry on top and putting it in the oven to bake.

1 tablespoon extra-virgin olive oil

1 white onion, sliced

600 g (1 lb 5 oz) stewing beef, roughly diced

200 g (7 oz) Swiss brown mushrooms, quartered

¼ teaspoon freshly grated nutmeg

1 teaspoon ground cumin

1 × 400 g (14 oz) tin chopped tomatoes

1 tablespoon worcestershire sauce

1 teaspoon wholegrain mustard

300 ml (10 fl oz) beef or vegetable stock

1 tablespoon cornflour (cornstarch)

salt flakes and freshly ground black pepper

1 frozen butter puff pastry sheet, thawed

1 free-range egg, beaten

Heat the oil in a large saucepan over a medium heat, add the onion and cook for 2 minutes until just starting to soften. Add the beef pieces and brown on all sides, then add the mushrooms and spices and cook, stirring, for a further 5 minutes. Add the tomatoes, worcestershire sauce, mustard and stock and stir everything together, then bring to a simmer and cook over a medium–low heat for 1½ hours or until the meat is nice and tender with a gravy-like consistency.

Mix the cornflour together with 2 tablespoons water in a measuring cup to make a paste, then stir into the pan with the beef. Reduce the heat to low and simmer gently for five minutes until the sauce has thickened enough to coat the back of a spoon. Season to taste, remove from the heat and leave to cool slightly.

Preheat the oven to 180°C (350°F/Gas 4).

Pour the beef mixture into a 30 x 22 x 5 cm (12 x 8¾ x 2 in) pie dish and nestle a pie bird, if you have one, in the centre. Cut a cross in the middle of the pastry sheet and gently place the pastry over the dish so that the bird pokes out of the hole in the middle. Seal the edges, brush the pastry all over with the beaten egg wash and bake in the oven for 30–35 minutes or until the pastry is golden and flaky. Serve with mashed potato, pumpkin or sweet potato.

Chicken & leek pie

SERVES 4 PLUS LEFTOVERS

> **MRS** Who doesn't love a chicken pie? I use chicken thighs rather than breast in mine as the meat doesn't dry out when cooked for a long time. If you're not a fan of leeks you could always try using other veggies such as sweet corn, broccoli or mushroom here instead – we like to serve this one with steamed carrots tossed with feta, almonds and lemon olive oil.

2 tablespoons extra-virgin olive oil, plus extra for brushing

1 red onion, sliced

2 leeks, white and light green parts only, sliced

2 garlic cloves, thinly sliced

3 thyme sprigs, leaves only

500 g (1 lb 2 oz) free-range boneless, skinless chicken thighs, cut into 2–3 cm (¾–1¼ in) chunks

250 ml (8½ fl oz/1 cup) almond milk or regular milk

1 tablespoon cornflour (cornstarch)

1 × 400 g (14 oz) tin cannellini (lima) beans, drained

salt flakes and freshly ground black pepper

1 frozen butter puff pastry sheet, thawed

Heat the olive oil in a large heavy-based saucepan, add the onion and leeks and cook for 3–4 minutes until the veggies are just starting to soften. Add the garlic and thyme and cook for a further 2 minutes, then add the chicken pieces and cook for 2–3 minutes, stirring, until browned on all sides.

Stir the milk and cornflour together in a measuring cup, pour the mixture into the pan and bring to the boil, then reduce the heat and simmer for 5 minutes, until the sauce has thickened to a gravy-like consistency. Stir in the cannellini beans and season with salt and pepper, then remove from the heat and spoon into a 30 x 22 x 5 cm (12 x 8¾ x 2 in) pie dish.

Lay the puff pastry sheet over the pie dish, brush it with a little olive oil and prick a few holes in it with a fork, then transfer to the oven and bake for 50–60 minutes, or until the pastry is golden and nicely flaky. Serve.

TIP *I also like to make this pie with left-over roast chicken (page 140) – using the same quantity of meat but not adding it until the end with the cannellini beans. If you do the same, just be careful not to over-season the mixture as you won't need quite so much seasoning.*

Cottage pie

SERVES 4 PLUS LEFTOVERS

> **MRS** We usually make a version of this whenever we have left-over mashed potato around, varying the vegetable depending on what we have to hand and what's in season. Our secret ingredient is Mr Wilkinson's brown sauce but of course you could always make it without, or add a spoonful of tomato chutney instead.

2 tablespoons extra-virgin olive oil

1 red onion, diced

1 carrot, diced

2 small zucchini (courgettes), diced

500 g (1 lb 2 oz) lean minced (ground) beef

375 ml (12½ fl oz/1½ cups) beef or vegetable stock

1 tablespoon worcestershire sauce

2 tablespoons Mr Wilkinson's brown sauce (page 238)

1 tablespoon tomato paste (concentrated purée)

pinch of salt flakes

pinch of freshly ground black pepper

60 g (2 oz) grated cheddar

steamed peas and corn cobs, to serve

MASH TOPPING

750 g (1 lb 11 oz) all-purpose potatoes, cut into rough chunks

50 g (1¾ oz) salted butter

3 tablespoons milk

1 free-range egg

Preheat the oven to 180°C (350°F/Gas 4).

Get your mash topping started first. Place the potato pieces in a saucepan and cover with cold water. Bring to the boil over a high heat and cook for 20 minutes, or until the potatoes are soft and can be easily pierced with the point of a sharp knife.

Meanwhile, in a separate large heavy-based saucepan, heat the olive oil over a medium heat. Add the onion, carrot and zucchini and cook for 3–4 minutes until slightly softened, then add the minced beef. Use a wooden spoon to break up the meat into small pieces and cook, stirring, for 8–10 minutes until browned all over. Add the stock and bring to the boil, then add the worcestershire sauce, brown sauce, tomato paste, salt and pepper. Stir to combine, reduce the heat to low and leave to cook for 10 minutes, stirring occasionally, until most of the liquid has evaporated (if the meat looks like it is in danger of drying out completely just add a splash of water from the kettle). Remove from the heat, transfer to a 30 x 22 x 5 cm (12 x 8¾ x 2 in) pie dish and set aside.

Once the potatoes are cooked, turn off the heat and drain the potatoes, then return them to the pan and leave it on the hot hob to dry out. Using a potato ricer or masher, mash the potatoes until smooth then whisk in the butter, milk and egg.

Spread the mash evenly over the top of the minced beef, making sure the whole top is covered. Sprinkle over the cheese and bake in the oven for 30 minutes until lightly golden on top with the filling bubbling up underneath. Remove from the oven and leave to stand for a few minutes before serving with steamed peas and corn cobs.

Fish pie

SERVES 4 PLUS LEFTOVERS

> **MR** Ah, fish pie. I can kind of remember watching my first cooking show, I think it was Gary Rhodes or Rick Stein, and they were making one – it looked amazing. We love this in our household, though I don't add the chopped herbs to the sauce any more as the kids, for some reason, won't eat green flecks (the little buggers). Oh, and it should go without saying but a fish pie needs to have lots of big chunks of fish in it, so don't skimp here.

1 litre (34 fl oz/4 cups) water

1 kg (2 lb 3 oz) white fish fillets (I use rockling or flathead), cut into 3–4 cm (1¼ in–1½ in) chunks

3 tablespoons extra-virgin olive oil

1 celery stalk, diced

1 carrot, diced

1 white onion, diced

1 small fennel bulb, sliced

90 g (3 oz/ ⅓ cup) salted butter

90 g (3 oz) plain (all-purpose) flour

250 ml (8½ fl oz/1 cup) milk

zest and juice of 1 lemon

salt flakes and cracked black pepper

1 tablespoon each chopped dill and parsley

MASH TOPPING

750 g (1 lb 11 oz) all-purpose potatoes, cut into rough chunks

50 g (1¾ oz) salted butter

3 tablespoons milk

1 free-range egg

Preheat the oven to 180°C (350°F/Gas 4).

Get your mash topping started first. Place the potato pieces in a saucepan and cover with cold water. Bring to the boil over a high heat and cook for 20 minutes, or until the potatoes are soft and can be easily pierced with the point of a sharp knife. Turn off the heat and drain the potatoes, then return them to the pan and leave it on the hob to dry out. Using a potato ricer or masher, mash the potatoes until smooth, then whisk in the butter, milk and egg. Set aside.

Meanwhile, bring 1 litre (34 fl oz/4 cups) water to the boil in a large saucepan. Add the fish pieces, remove from the heat and leave to poach for 5 minutes. Carefully remove the fish using a slotted spoon and set aside on a plate, then strain the poaching liquor (you've just made a fish stock!) and measure out 500 ml (17 fl oz/ 2 cups), saving the remainder for soups or risottos.

Heat the olive oil in a large saucepan over a medium heat, add the celery, carrot, onion and fennel and sauté for 5 minutes until softened. Increase the heat to high, add the butter and, once melted, stir in the flour. Cook for 2–3 minutes, stirring, to form a paste (roux). Reduce the heat to medium then add the fish stock and milk a few ladlefuls at a time, stirring all the while, until all the liquid has been added and the sauce is thick enough to coat the back of a wooden spoon. Remove from the heat, add the lemon juice and zest and season to taste, then stir in the chopped herbs.

Pour the sauce into a 30 x 22 x 5 cm (12 x 8¾ x 2 in) pie dish, arrange the fish pieces over the top and mix them into the sauce gently. Spread the mash carefully over the top (you could pipe this on if you're feeling cheffy, though I wouldn't bother), then pop the pie into the oven and bake for 30 minutes, or until the potato is nicely browned on top. Serve.

Bacon & egg pie

SERVES 4 PLUS LEFTOVERS

> **MRS** This is a super-easy dinner to cook on the fly. We give our chickens our kitchen scraps and they give us eggs most days, so whenever we get a surplus this is a great way to use up them up.

extra-virgin olive oil, for brushing

1 frozen butter puff pastry sheet, thawed

6 free-range eggs

4 free-range bacon rashers, roughly chopped

200 g (7 oz) cauliflower, cut in small florets

100 ml (3½ fl oz) milk

60 g (2 oz/ ½ cup) grated cheddar

pinch of salt flakes

½ tablespoon finely chopped parsley (optional)

½ tablespoon finely chopped chives (optional)

Mr Wilkinson's red sauce, to serve (page 240)

Preheat the oven to 180°C (350°F/Gas 4). Brush a 30 x 22 x 5 cm (12 x 8¾ x 2 in) pie dish with olive oil.

Line the oiled pie dish with the puff pastry sheet, then brush the pastry with oil and prick the base all over with a fork. Bake for 10 minutes until the pastry is risen but still pale, then remove the tin from the oven and press the pastry down with your fingers to flatten.

While your pastry is par-cooking, whisk the eggs together in a bowl. Add the bacon, cauliflower, milk, cheese, salt and chopped herbs, if using, and stir to combine.

Pour the filling into the pre-baked pastry and bake for 20–25 minutes, or until the filling is cooked through and has just set with no wobbly bits. Serve warm or cold with the red sauce.

Zucchini slice

SERVES 4 PLUS LEFTOVERS

> **MRS** We make plenty of these in the summer when we have a glut of zucchini. When cold it cuts into solid chunks and holds together well for the lunchbox.

4 small zucchini (courgettes), grated

pinch of salt flakes

1 white onion, finely diced

4 free-range bacon rashers, roughly chopped

75 g (2¾ oz/ ½ cup) self-raising flour

5 free-range eggs

125 ml (4 fl oz/ ½ cup) milk

80 g (2¾ oz) grated cheddar (use more or less as you prefer)

2 vine-ripened tomatoes, sliced

2 tablespoons pepitas (pumpkin seeds) (optional)

Preheat the oven to 180°C (350°F/Gas 4). Line a 25 x 25 x 6 cm (10 x 10 x 2 in) baking tin with baking paper.

Add the grated zucchini and salt to a colander and mix together well. Squeeze out the zucchini over the sink to remove any excess moisture, then transfer to a bowl together with the onion, bacon and flour and mix well.

In a separate small bowl, beat the eggs together well, add the milk and whisk to combine. Pour the egg mixture into the zucchini, add half the cheese and stir to combine.

Pour the mixture into the prepared baking tin. Lay the sliced tomatoes over the top in a random pattern and sprinkle over the pepitas, if using, then scatter over the rest of the cheese. Bake for 40–50 minutes, until the slice is cooked through and the cheese on top is browned.

Remove from the oven and leave to rest for 10 minutes before cutting. Serve warm or cold on its own or with steamed veggies or a green salad. The slice will keep in an airtight container for up to 3 days in the fridge.

Freeform potato & cheese pie

SERVES 4

> **MR** When I first came to Melbourne in 2004 I volunteered at Stephanie Alexander's Kitchen Garden Foundation program in the kitchen at Collingwood College where it all started. Now they have over 800 schools and early learning centres participating in the program in different ways across Australia. This recipe was from one of the original teachers on staff there and we were teaching grade 3s to make it, so anyone can have a crack at it and get great results. You need potato as the base filling but can add extra veggies and herbs as you like.

4 all-purpose potatoes, cut into 4–5 cm (1½–2 in) chunks

300 g (10½ oz/2 cups) plain (all-purpose) flour

160 g (5½ oz/⅔ cup) salted butter, cut into 1 cm (½ in) cubes

2 free-range eggs, lightly beaten

1 white onion, finely sliced

50 g (1¾ oz) cream cheese

65 g (2¼ oz) grated cheddar or Swiss cheese

1 tablespoon sweet chilli sauce

1 handful soft herbs (such as parsley, tarragon or chives), finely chopped (optional)

1 tablespoon milk

salad leaves, to serve

Place the potato pieces in a saucepan and cover with cold water. Bring to the boil over a high heat and cook for 20 minutes until soft.

While the potato is cooking, prepare the pastry. Place the flour in a large bowl, add the butter and rub in with your fingertips until the mixture resembles rough breadcrumbs. Add the egg little by little to form a soft dough, saving a smidgen of egg for brushing the pastry later. Turn the dough out onto a floured work surface and knead until smooth, then wrap in baking paper, transfer to the fridge and leave for 30 minutes to firm.

Preheat the oven to 180°C (350°F/Gas 4) and line a baking tray with baking paper.

Once the potatoes are cooked, drain them in a colander and place in a bowl. Add the onion and cream cheese and mix together gently with a wooden spoon (you want to keep the potato as lumps rather than mash), then stir through the grated cheese, chilli sauce and herbs.

Remove the pastry from the fridge and roll it out on a floured work surface into a rough circle about 5 mm (¼ in) thick. Spoon the potato filling into the centre of the pastry leaving a border of 5 cm (2 in) around the outside, then fold the sides up towards the centre to form the edges (the pastry won't cover the pie completely and can be rough and uneven – it doesn't need to look perfect).

Combine the milk and left-over beaten egg and use it to brush over the exposed pastry, then bake for 30 minutes, until the pastry is golden and flaky. Serve with a green salad.

Roast chicken

SERVES 4

The roast chicken is probably the king of leftovers. Here is my how-to-roast method and recipe plus my favourite things to do with the leftovers.

MR There are many recipes for cooking a chicken, and this version differs a little from my first book as I have been slowly tweaking my cooking methods. Too many people overcook chicken, I think worried about undercooking and seeing blood, but a little bit of pink in a chicken is ok and doesn't always mean it is undercooked. For a larger (or smaller) bird than this I add (or subtract) 5 minutes of cooking time for every 200 g (7 oz) of weight. Oh, and there's no need to truss. Truss me ... (sorry, Dad joke!). After the meal I pick off whatever meat is left over and use it for the next few days, as well as separating the wings from the carcass and freezing both to make my Golden chicken soup (page 141) later down the line.

1 × 1.8 kg (4 lb) free-range whole chicken

50 g (1¾ oz) salted butter, cut into 2 rectangular slabs

2 tarragon sprigs (optional, could be thyme or any herb you like really)

1 garlic bulb, cut in half

Preheat the oven to 250°C (480°F/Gas 9).

Loosen the skin from the neck end of the chicken, then work the butter slabs and herb sprigs under it to cover the breasts, dividing them between sides. Stuff the garlic bulb halves into the cavity.

Put the chicken in a roasting tin and roast for 20 minutes, then turn the oven down to 190°C (375°F/Gas 5) and cook for a further 25 minutes until golden. Turn off the oven and leave the chicken to rest inside for 10 minutes, then transfer to a wooden board for carving. Serve.

Golden chicken soup

SERVES 2

MR I love this soup so much that sometimes I even make it without leftovers (see Tip below). It's a recipe adapted from Andrew McConnell during my time at Circa but I adjusted the cooking method after seeing how the lovely Christine Manfield cooked her Asian broths. I like to serve it with Sharlee's home-made wontons or little pork meatballs (see pages 160) or sliced beef and bok choy (pak choy) with soba noodles or rice vermicelli, but it's also lovely just on its own. It's also great if you're feeling unwell – just add a bit more garlic and ginger.

1 left-over roast chicken carcass, wings separated and cooking fat reserved

6 cm (2½ in) piece fresh ginger, skin on and thinly sliced

2 tablespoons sesame oil

70 ml (2¼ fl oz) rice vinegar

100 ml (3½ fl oz) soy sauce

2 × 4 cm (1½ in) pieces kombu (optional)

3 spring onions (scallions), chopped into 4 equal-sized parts

8 garlic cloves

your choice of wontons, pork meatballs, beef slices, bok choy (pak choy), soba noodles or rice vermicelli, to serve (optional)

Preheat the oven to 180°C (350°F/Gas 4).

Add the chicken carcass, wings and any left over cooking fat from the initial roasting to a tin and roast for 12–15 minutes until golden.

Transfer the left-over chicken carcass and chicken wings to a large bowl set over a large saucepan of boiling water (or use a double boiler). Add the remaining ingredients to the bowl and cover with foil and leave to cook for 1–1½ hours, checking the saucepan below and adding more water if needed, until silky and intensely flavoured. Strain, discarding the chicken pieces and all the other flavourings and serve on its own or with your choice of accompaniments.

TIP *To make this without leftovers, roast an uncooked chicken carcass and 4 chicken wings in an oven preheated to 220°C (430°F/Gas 7) for 15–17 minutes until golden, then leave to cool and proceed as described.*

Cornish sandwich

SERVES 2

MR This famous sandwich has been on the menu since day one at Pope Joan and is named after my friend, the food writer and gorgeous giant of a man Richard Cornish. It's great with a cold beer, while the filling also works brilliantly in a baked potato with cheese.

200 g (7 oz) left-over roast chicken meat, roughly chopped

3 tablespoons Mayo (page 245)

6 brine-pickled jalapenos, chopped, plus 2 tablespoons brine

salt flakes and freshly ground black pepper

2 soft bread rolls or hot dog rolls

4 cos (romaine) lettuce leaves

Mix together the chicken, mayo, jalapeno and brine in a bowl and season to your taste with salt and pepper. Heat a frying pan over a medium heat, spoon the chicken mixture into the pan and fry for 2–3 minutes, stirring, until warmed through. Divide between rolls, add the cos leaves and enjoy with a cold beer.

We have two beautiful chickens at home, Bryan and Major, named by Finn, our eldest. One day before we got them Finn and I were doing a bit of gardening and I said to him, 'Matey, you know the two chickens we are getting are hens that lay eggs and hens are female, so they're girls right? Bryan and Major are kinda boys, names.' Finn's reply was, 'Yeah Dad, I know, and I also know that when they stop laying eggs you're going to kill them and we are going to eat them because Mum told me. But we're not, Dad, alright!'

Brown rice salad

SERVES 2

MR As a kid, Mum's brown rice, tuna and corn was, well, sorry Mum ... horrible. Luckily it didn't put me off brown rice completely though, which is just as well as it is now a go-to ingredient in our home, whether served up as a side or made into a simple, delicious salad like this. This is a great one to pop into containers and take to work for lunch – to bulk it out throw in some cooked broccoli, zucchini, Asian greens or pumpkin, or even some raw carrot.

150 g (5½ oz/ ¾ cup) brown rice

200 g (7 oz) left-over roast chicken meat, chopped

100 g (3½ oz/ ½ cup) kimchi, chopped (optional)

1 tablespoon extra-virgin olive oil

1 tablespoon soy sauce

chilli sauce, to serve

Rinse the rice under cold water then place in a saucepan together with 1 litre (34 fl oz/4 cups) water. Bring to the boil, then reduce to a simmer and cook for 20 minutes, or until tender. Strain, then transfer to a bowl together with all the remaining ingredients and mix together well. Divide between bowls and serve.

A NOTE ON ETHICAL AND SUSTAINABLE MEAT FROM MATT ...

The unfortunate reality of life is that we all die and that animals have to die for us to eat them. So, surely, if we are to eat something, we should want it to have the best life it can until death. This is one of the two main reasons I choose ethical meat. The other important factor for me is that the meat that I have tried that has been raised in this way tastes so much better because those who work in this area show their love in every aspect of their business – from choosing the right pasture, rearing and breeding, to the transportation and kill process and, finally, the butchery and delivery of the final product. They know every step of the chain in their business and that's why I support local farmers direct from the source (and in doing so I have gained some amazing knowledge and friends).

When it comes to sustainable, ethically sourced meat (and fruit and veg too for that matter) the question of price often comes up. All I am going to say is that a kilo of quality meat can set you back from $14 for, say, mince to $45 for prime steak, while a kilo of Mars bars will cost you $37. Go figure. My best advice would be to buy from someone you trust and do your research, asking questions of your food providers not just at the butcher's or the market but also at the cafes and restaurants you go to, wherever you get your food from. Get the answers and then make your choice – it's how we live our lives at home and at work. For more on this, check out the sustainable table website (www.sustainable.org.au) and head to the Hungry For Info section to learn more.

Our Weekly Dinners

MRS

The golden rule for dinner is be prepared, as there is nothing worse than finding it's 5 pm and you haven't worked out what's on the menu. In a perfect world I do a weekly meal plan on a Sunday, checking what's in the garden, freezer and cupboard that needs to be used first.

Of course, we have our core repertoire of recipes we cook a lot that make up the basis of our weekly dinners, but we also like to mix it up by trying out new recipes too. We have an extraordinary number of cookbooks between us and found that we rarely cooked from them so we instigated a little plan a few years ago that I pick a book and then Matt picks a recipe from that book for me to cook and vice versa. It works really well and has widened our home repertoire as a result.

This chapter is a snapshot of a random weekly menu, complete with easy dishes and some that take a bit more prep. Some days I may do most of the cooking in the morning and then simply heat the dish up later because we have after-school activities on and don't get home until late. Whatever the day though, we always have dinner spot-on at 6 pm, which is when Matt gets home from Pope Joan. We all sit at the table together to talk about our day and the things that made us happy. It's a great way to connect and engage with each other and we hope it fosters in the boys a real appreciation for meal times.

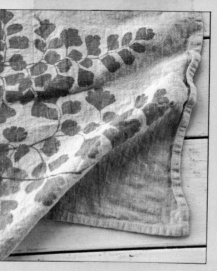

Bibimbap

SERVES 4

> **MRS** Bibimbap is a Korean dish that translates as 'mixing rice', and is usually topped with beef and vegetables. This is one of our favourite meals for throwing together on a weeknight as we can use whatever we have in the fridge.

1 tablespoon soy sauce

1 teaspoon sesame oil

½ pear, grated

4 cm (1½ in) piece fresh ginger, grated

1 garlic clove, crushed

1 teaspoon raw (demerara) sugar

300 g (10½ oz) beef steak (skirt, flank or hanger), cut into thin strips

200 g (7 oz/1 cup) jasmine rice, rinsed in cold water

80 ml (2½ fl oz/ ⅓ cup) extra-virgin olive oil

1 carrot, cut into thin matchsticks

1 teaspoon sesame oil

1 teaspoon black sesame seeds

1 zucchini (courgette), sliced diagonally

1 corn cob, kernels removed

1 tablespoon soy sauce

1 teaspoon honey

1 handful leafy greens, thick stalks removed

1 tablespoon kecap manis

4 free-range eggs

TO SERVE

kimchi/sauerkraut/pickles and chopped cashew nuts, to serve (optional)

Make the marinade by mixing the soy sauce, sesame oil, grated pear, ginger, garlic and sugar together in a bowl. Add the beef strips and leave to marinate for 30 minutes.

Add the rice and 375 ml (12½ fl oz/1½ cups) water to a saucepan over a high heat, cover with a lid and bring to the boil. Once boiling, remove the lid and stir, then reduce the heat to a simmer and cook, covered, for 20 minutes. Remove from the heat and leave to sit, still covered, for 10 minutes.

Meanwhile, heat 1 tablespoon of the olive oil in a large frying pan or wok over a high heat. Add the marinated beef and cook, tossing to ensure it cooks evenly, for 3–4 minutes. Remove from the pan and transfer to a warm plate.

Add another tablespoon of olive oil to the pan together with the carrot matchsticks and sesame oil. Cook, tossing, for 2–3 minutes, then remove from the pan, sprinkle with the sesame seeds and keep warm. Add another 1 tablespoon olive oil to the pan, throw in the zucchini and stir-fry for 2–3 minutes, then add the corn kernels, soy sauce and honey. Stir-fry for 2 minutes then remove from the pan and keep warm as before.

Add another tablespoon of olive oil to the pan, throw in the leafy greens and the kecap manis and stir-fry for 1–2 minutes, then remove from the pan and keep warm. (Rinse the pan with water to remove any residue.) Lastly, add the final tablespoon of olive oil, making sure the pan is hot and break the eggs separately into the pan. Fry for 3–5 minutes to your liking, then remove from the heat.

Build your bibimbap bowls starting with the rice on the bottom, then adding the beef and vegetables around the bowl as separate components. Add condiments like kimchi, sauerkraut or pickles and scatter over some chopped cashew nuts if you like (I do). Add a fried egg to each bowl and serve.

TIP *If you like chilli, try putting a little gochujang (Korean red chilli paste) on the top of your bowl when serving.*

Turkey not-so-chilli

SERVES 4

> **MRS** This is comfort food at its best. Minced turkey doesn't have the fat content of minced pork or beef, but this is balanced out by the sweet potato purée. I always make sure there are leftovers for the next day.

2 tablespoons extra-virgin olive oil

1 sweet potato, roughly chopped

2 garlic cloves, roughly chopped

pinch of cayenne pepper, plus extra if necessary

2 teaspoons ground coriander

2 teaspoons ground cumin

2 teaspoons sweet paprika

500 ml (17 fl oz/2 cups) vegetable or chicken stock

1 red onion, finely diced

500 g (1 lb 2 oz) minced (ground) turkey

1 × 400 g (14 oz) tin cannellini (lima) beans, drained

1 teaspoon apple-cider vinegar

salt flakes and freshly ground black pepper

TO SERVE

sour cream

coriander (cilantro) leaves

lime wedges

corn tortilla chips

Heat 1 tablespoon of the olive oil in a large saucepan over a medium heat. Add the sweet potato and garlic and cook for 1–2 minutes, then add the cayenne and 1 teaspoon each of the coriander, cumin and paprika. Cook for a further 1–2 minutes, tossing the sweet potato in the pan to coat it evenly in the spices, then pour over the stock to cover (if you need a little more liquid then top it up with water from the kettle) and bring to the boil. Once boiling, reduce the heat to a simmer and cook for 10–15 minutes, or until the sweet potato is soft, then transfer everything to a food processor and blitz to a smooth purée. Set aside.

Return the pan to the heat, add the remaining olive oil together with the red onion and sauté for 3–4 minutes over a medium heat. Add the turkey and remaining spices, using a wooden spoon to break the meat up into small pieces, and cook for 3–4 minutes until browned. Stir in the sweet potato purée, cannellini beans and apple-cider vinegar and season to taste, adding extra cayenne if you like things spicy. Reduce the heat to low and simmer gently for 5 minutes, adding a splash of water if the sauce becomes too dry.

Spoon the chilli into bowls and serve with sour cream, coriander leaves, fresh lime and corn chips for a Mexican vibe.

Stir-fried pork & rice

SERVES 4

> MRS With its gorgeous mix of salty and sweet, this is one of those great recipes that takes no time to cook and gets devoured by the kids. It's great served as it is, though if you want you could always top it with some sliced chillies, fresh herbs, crunchy toasted nuts or even a fried egg. The eggplant here can also be replaced with other stir-fried veg in season like zucchini, cabbage or green beans.

500 g (1 lb 2 oz) free-range minced (ground) pork

1 small eggplant, cut into 5 mm (¼ in) dice

2 tablespoons kecap manis

1 tablespoon soy sauce

200 g (7 oz/1 cup) jasmine rice, rinsed in cold water

2 tablespoons extra-virgin olive oil

juice of ¼ orange

Put the pork, eggplant, kecap manis and soy sauce in a bowl, and mix together with a fork. Cover with a plate, transfer to the fridge and leave to marinate for 2–3 hours (removing from the fridge 20 minutes prior to cooking to take the chill off).

Add the rice and 375 ml (12½ fl oz/1½ cups) water to a saucepan over a high heat, cover with a lid and bring to the boil. Once boiling, remove the lid and stir, then reduce the heat to a simmer and cook, covered, for 20 minutes. Remove from the heat and leave to sit, still covered, for 10 minutes.

Heat the olive oil in a large frying pan or wok, add the marinated pork mixture and sauté for 10 minutes, using a wooden spoon to break up the minced pork into small pieces as you go, until the pork is cooked through and the eggplant is soft. Add the cooked rice and orange juice and toss everything together. Serve.

A NOTE ON CHILLI SAUCE FROM MATT ...

If you are a couple and one of you likes chilli and the other doesn't it can become hard. I always omit chilli from foods and add it when serving, especially now we have kids. With most cuisines like Italian, Spanish and South American, Malaysian, Thai, Vietnamese and Chinese this works well, and our pantry and fridge are stocked with an array of easy-to-find chilli sauces from around the world for adding to the meal at the end like this. With Indian-style hot curries, where there is so much complexity in the spices used and in the slow cooking and braising, it is hard to omit the chilli. I now make these sorts of curries at home with hardly any spice so we can all enjoy them.

Lizette's veal schnitzel

SERVES 4

> **MR** Lizette and Allen Snaith are the cattle-breeding farmer duo behind Warialda Belted Galloways. Over the last few years I have spent many times with them on and off their farm and they have become dear friends to me. Lizette makes the best schnitzel ever I reckon – it's a mixture of the beef they use (theirs obviously), the method she uses to crumb it and the way she cooks it in plenty of foaming butter. It is a family tradition of hers, the recipe passed on from her grandmother.
>
> Lizette's grandmother 'Hansi' was born a Catholic in Czechoslovakia, raised in Austria and married an Austrian Jew. Together they fled Nazi Austria to Shanghai, where after the Japanese invasion she became a prisoner of war, arriving safely on the shores of Melbourne to set up home in 1946.

3 free-range eggs

3 tablespoons milk

150 g (5½ oz/1 cup) plain (all-purpose) flour

pinch of salt flakes

pinch of freshly ground black pepper

200 g (7 oz/2 cups) fine breadcrumbs

1 × 600 g (1 lb 5 oz) beef silverside (round steak), cut into 4–5 mm (¼ in) thick slices and sinews removed

150 g (5½ oz) salted butter

1 lemon, cut into wedges

A LITTLE NOTE FROM LIZETTE
We like to use the left-over crumbing bits to make a type of Kartoffelpuffer (a German pancake). To make it, add the left-over flour to the egg mixture, then beat in an extra egg and top up with milk until you have a nice thick consistency. Pour the mixture into the pan after cooking the schnitzel and fry for a few minutes on each side until golden. Cut into triangles to serve.

Whisk together the eggs and milk in a mixing bowl. In a separate bowl mix together the flour, salt and pepper.

Lay two good-sized pieces of baking paper on a work surface and put the seasoned flour on one and the breadcrumbs on the other. Place the bowl with the beaten egg next to them to create an assembly line in the following order from left to right: flour, then eggs, then breadcrumbs (this is the order you will crumb the meat in).

Take one steak piece and place it on top of the flour, pressing it down firmly using your knuckles. Turn it over to repeat, then dip the floured meat into the beaten egg, turning it over to ensure both sides are covered. Lay the meat over the breadcrumbs and press it down as before, then turn and repeat. Lift the schnitzel up and shake it gently to remove any excess crumbs, then set it aside and repeat the process with the remaining meat pieces.

Set a large heavy-based frying pan over a medium heat and add 50 g (1¾ oz) of the butter. Once the butter is foaming, add a schnitzel to the pan and cook for 2 minutes, or until the crumbs on the underside are golden. Turn the schnitzel over and cook another minute until golden all over, adding a little more butter if needed. Remove from the pan and repeat with the remaining schnitzels, adding a little butter as needed, until all the meat is cooked. Serve immediately with lemon wedges and a simple green salad.

Inauthentic tacos

SERVES 4

> **MRS** I know it's putting it out there, but I grew up on Old El Paso tacos and I love those hard taco shells. Back in the day we had them with lentils rather than minced beef, setting up the lazy Susan on the dinner table with all the accompaniments. I make my own taco seasoning these days but I'm still a sucker for the hard shell.

FILLING

1 tablespoon extra-virgin olive oil

1 red onion, finely chopped

1 garlic clove, finely diced

500 g (1 lb 2 oz) minced (ground) beef

1 teaspoon each of sweet paprika, cumin and ground coriander

1 × 400 g (14 oz) tin chopped tomatoes

1 carrot, grated

1 teaspoon red-wine vinegar

pinch of salt flakes

TOMATO SALSA

2–3 ripe tomatoes, roughly chopped

juice of ½ lime

pinch of salt flakes

1 handful coriander (cilantro) leaves, chopped

TO SERVE

Guacamole (see page 246)

125 g (4½ oz/1 cup) grated cheddar

125 g (4½ oz/ ½ cup) natural yoghurt

½ iceberg, cos (romaine) or butter lettuce, shredded

12 hard taco shells

Preheat the oven to 180°C (350°F/Gas 4).

For the filling, heat the olive oil in a large saucepan over a medium heat, add the onion and garlic and cook for 1–2 minutes until just softened. Add the beef and spices, using a wooden spoon to break the meat up into small pieces, and cook for 3–4 minutes until browned. Add the chopped tomatoes, carrot, red-wine vinegar and salt and cook for a further 10–15 minutes until the mince is cooked through and most of the liquid has been absorbed.

While the mince is cooking, prepare the accompaniments. For the tomato salsa, put all the ingredients in a bowl and mix together well, then transfer to the fridge until needed. For the guacamole, see page 246. Put the cheese, yoghurt and lettuce in separate bowls.

Place the taco shells in the oven for 5–6 minutes to warm.

Once ready to serve, ladle the filling into a large bowl. Place the taco shells and all the accompaniments in the centre of the table (a lazy Susan comes in handy here) and dig in. Warning – this gets messy!

Prawn dumplings with Asian greens

SERVES 4 (MAKES ABOUT 35 DUMPLINGS)

> **MRS** There's a moment of satisfaction when you realise you can make dumplings at home for yourself. While it does take time to fill and fold them you'll soon get in the flow – just set up a production line and you'll be pushing out a PB in no time.

350 g (12½ oz) raw prawns (shrimp), peeled and deveined

1 tablespoon grated fresh ginger

1 tablespoon soy sauce

2 teaspoons sesame oil

pinch of salt flakes

1 x 250 g (9 oz) packet square wonton wrappers

1 × Fried rice (page 191), to serve

ASIAN GREENS

10 snake beans, chopped into thirds

2 bok choy (pak choy) stems, trimmed and leaves separated

3 tablespoons garlic-infused olive oil

1 tablespoon sesame seeds

2 tablespoons oyster sauce

Put the prawns, ginger, soy sauce, sesame oil and salt in a food processor and pulse to form a chunky paste.

Lay a wrapper out on a clean work surface and place a teaspoon of the prawn mixture in the centre. Brush the edges of the wrapper lightly with water then fold over one side on a diagonal to form a triangle. Press to seal at the top, then continue to push down and seal from the left to the right, making sure to remove any air bubbles. Finally, grab the two bottom corners of the triangle and bring them together around the filling, pressing tightly to form the dumpling shape. (The shape is technically a tortellini fold but it's easy to learn – if you find the filling is bulging out when you are folding the triangle over, try reducing the amount of filling you use.) Repeat with the remaining wonton wrappers and filling until all the filling has been used up.

Layer two bamboo steamer baskets with baking paper and bring a saucepan one-third filled with water to the boil. Place the dumplings in the baskets, then set them over the pan and cover with a lid. Cook for 10–15 minutes, or until the dumplings are offer a little resistance when pressed.

For the Asian greens, bring a saucepan of water to the boil and heat a frying pan or wok over a high heat until smoking. Blanch the snake beans and bok choy in the boiling water for 20 seconds, then drain and toss into the frying pan with the garlic oil, sesame seeds and 1 tablespoon of the oyster sauce for 30 seconds. Transfer to a plate and drizzle over the remaining oyster sauce.

Remove the cooked dumpling from the steamer baskets and serve with the Asian greens and Fried rice (page 191).

Rissoles with sugo

SERVES 4

> **MRS** These old school meatballs are a guaranteed crowd-pleaser that come with the added bonus of packing some veg. You can make them gluten free by replacing the breadcrumbs with an alternative – I used seaweed rice crackers one time and they worked really well.

1 small red onion, finely diced

1 carrot, grated

1 zucchini (courgette), grated

100 g (3½ oz) free-range rindless bacon, finely diced

250 g (9 oz) free-range minced (ground) pork

250 g (9 oz) minced (ground) veal

40 g (1½ oz/ ½ cup) fresh breadcrumbs

1 teaspoon fennel seeds

1 teaspoon salt flakes

1 free-range egg, beaten

2–3 tablespoons extra-virgin olive oil

1 x quantity Polenta (page 246) and parmesan cheese, grated, to serve

SUGO

2 tablespoons extra-virgin olive oil

1 white onion, sliced

1 garlic clove, sliced

1 × 400 g (14 oz) tinned chopped tomatoes or fresh tomatoes, diced

½ teaspoon salt flakes

1 teaspoon balsamic vinegar

1 handful basil leaves, torn (optional)

Preheat the oven to 180°C (350°F/Gas 4).

Put the onion, carrot, zucchini and bacon in a large bowl, add the minced pork and veal, breadcrumbs, fennel and salt and mix everything together with your hands until well combined. Stir the beaten egg into the mince with a fork, then take tablespoonfuls of the mixture and shape into balls (you can make these larger if you like but be aware that they will take a few more minutes to cook). Arrange the rissoles on a baking tray and refrigerate for 30 minutes to chill and firm.

While the rissoles are chilling, make the sugo. Heat the olive oil in a pan over a medium heat, add the onion and garlic and cook, stirring, for 2–3 minutes until softened. Stir in the tomatoes, salt and balsamic vinegar, bring to a simmer and cook for a further 15 minutes until thickened and reduced. Season to taste and stir in the basil leaves if using. Keep warm until ready to serve.

Heat 1 tablespoon of olive oil in a frying pan over a medium–high heat. Being sure not to overcrowd the pan, cook the rissoles in batches for 2–3 minutes on all sides until lightly browned, using tongs to turn them as you go and adding a little more oil between each batch as needed. Once browned, transfer the rissoles to a large deep baking tray, spacing them out evenly, and pour over the sugo to cover. Bake in the oven for 30 minutes.

Meanwhile, make the polenta (page 246).

Serve the polenta wet and runny and cover with a generous ladleful of rissoles and sugo. Scatter over a little grated parmesan cheese to finish.

Bolognese

SERVES 4

Bolognese could quite possibly be the most cooked dish in the world, so surely that also makes it a contender for the one that is most often left over. Here's my way of making it along with some lip-smackingly good things to do with the leftovers.

MR For me a mixture of veal and pork delivers a bolognese with the best flavour, though a straight-up beef-only one made from meat with a 15% fat content runs a close second. My good friend and ex–head chef of Pope Joan, Jason Newton, puts cinnamon sticks, chilli, whole oranges or mandarins and star anise in his – craaazy. Nice chilli con carne, Jase.

200 g (7 oz) minced (ground) veal

200 g (7 oz) free-range minced (ground) pork

5 garlic cloves, chopped

75 ml (2½ fl oz) extra-virgin olive oil

1 carrot, finely diced

1 red onion, finely diced

2 tablespoons tomato paste (concentrated purée)

1 tablespoon red-wine vinegar

½ tablespoon sugar

salt flakes and freshly ground black pepper

1 × 400 g (14 oz) tin chopped tomatoes or home-made Sugo (page 160)

1 × 50 g (1¾ oz) parmesan rind (optional)

3 basil stalks (optional)

freshly grated parmesan, to serve

Place the veal and pork, garlic, oil, carrot and onion in a heavy-based saucepan over a high heat and cook for 5–6 minutes, until the meat has just started to brown and has softened. Stir in the tomato paste and cook for 2 minutes, stirring, then add the vinegar and sugar and season to taste. Add the chopped tomatoes or Sugo (page 160), 400 ml (13½ fl oz) water, parmesan rind and basil, if using, bring to a simmer and cook for 18–22 minutes, or until thickened and delicious. Discard the basil and parmesan rind and season. Serve with freshly grated parmesan cheese.

Stuffed baked potato wrapped in bacon

SERVES 2

> **MR** I love stuffing potatoes like this. It reminds me of when I first left home and was really quite poor, when I would make dinner out of anything.

2 large potatoes

100 g (3½ oz) Bolognese (page 162)

2 tablespoons sour cream

30 g (1 oz/ ¼ cup) grated cheddar

6 free-range bacon rashers

salad leaves, to serve

Preheat the oven to 220°C (430°F/Gas 7).

Prick the potatoes all over with a fork, then transfer to a microwave and cook on high for 8 minutes. Remove from the microwave, transfer to the oven and cook for a further 8 minutes. Alternatively, cook in the oven only for 35–45 minutes).

Reduce the oven temperature to 200°C (400°F/Gas 6).

Leave the potatoes to cool, then cut them in half and scoop out three-quarters of the flesh from each half into a bowl. Using a potato ricer or masher, mash the potatoes until smooth, then add half the mash to a bowl with the Bolognese, sour cream and cheese (use the remaining mashed potato for fishcakes). Mix together well.

Spoon the mash mixture into the potato halves, then sandwich the filled halves back together and wrap with the bacon rashers. Place on a baking tray and bake for 22–26 minutes, or until the bacon is nice and crispy. Serve with salad.

Cheesy bolognese on garlic bread

SERVES 2–4

MR One of my closest friends, 'old man' Steve Rogers, came up with this idea and it is, quite frankly, genius.

3 garlic cloves, crushed

1 tablespoon salt flakes

45 g (1½ oz) unsalted butter, softened

1 tablespoon chopped parsley

1 demi baguette, halved lengthways

100 g (3½ oz) Bolognese (page 162)

100 g (3½ oz) grated cheddar

chilli sauce, to serve (optional)

Preheat the oven to 190°C (375°F/Gas 5).

Mix together the garlic, salt, softened butter and parsley in a bowl with a fork until well combined.

Smear the cut sides of the baguette halves with the garlic butter, then sandwich the two halves back together. Wrap the baguette in aluminium foil and bake in the oven for 8 minutes.

Remove the baguette from the oven and unwrap and separate the halves. Smear the bolognese evenly over both and scatter over the cheese, then return to the oven and cook for a further 7–9 minutes, or until the cheese has melted. Remove from the oven, cut into pieces and top with a splash or two of chilli sauce, if you like. Boom.

Croquettes

MAKES 15

50 g (1¾ oz) salted butter

40 g (1½ oz/ ¼ cup) plain (all-purpose) flour

1 teaspoon cornflour (cornstarch)

300 ml (10 fl oz) milk, plus 2 tablespoons for coating

200 g (7 oz) Bolognese (page 162)

40 g (1½ oz/ ⅓ cup) grated cheddar

1 free-range egg

35 g (1¼ oz/ ¼ cup) plain (all-purpose) flour, for crumbing

50 g (1¾ oz/ ½ cup) dried fine breadcrumbs

non-GMO vegetable oil, for deep-frying

Melt the butter in a small saucepan over a medium heat, add the flour and cornflour and beat for 1 minute to form a paste (roux). Cook for 5–6 minutes, stirring all the while and adding the milk a few tablespoonfuls at a time, to form a smooth white sauce. Remove from the heat and stir through the bolognese and cheddar, then transfer to the fridge to cool.

Beat the egg together with the extra milk in a bowl. Place the flour in a separate bowl and add the breadcrumbs to a third bowl.

Divide the chilled croquette mixture into 15 equal-sized pieces and shape into balls. Roll one of the balls in the flour, dip it into the egg mixture to coat evenly then roll in the breadcrumbs until covered all over. Repeat with the remaining balls.

Half-fill a small saucepan with oil and bring to a temperature of 175°C (345°F), or until a cube of bread browns in 30 seconds. Gently lower the croquettes into the hot oil and cook for 4–6 minutes until golden. Remove with a slotted spoon and drain on kitchen paper, then eat straight away.

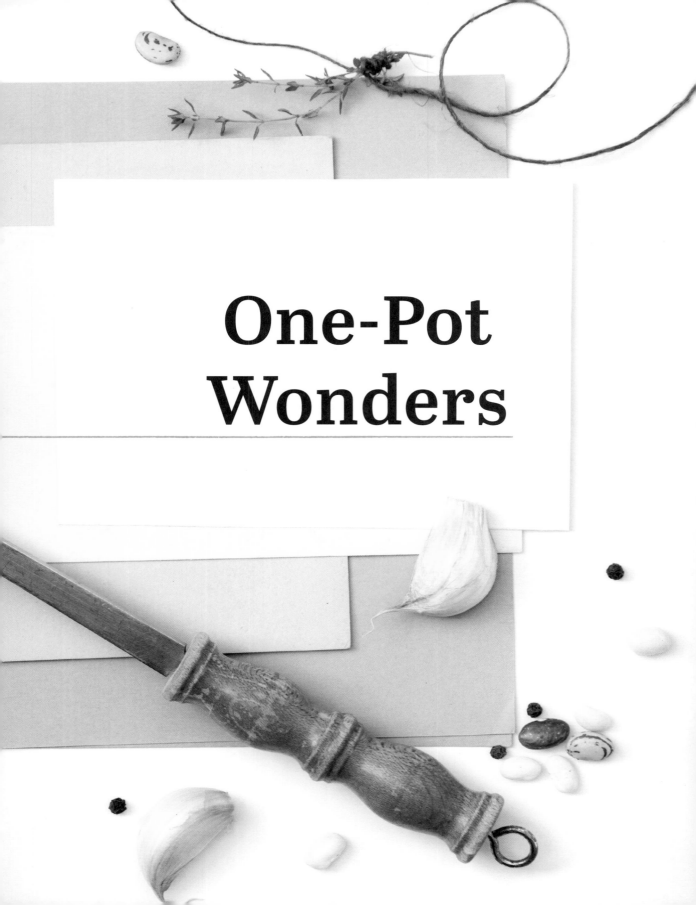

One-Pot
Wonders

MR I love one-pot cooking so much that at one point it was going to be the subject of my third book – that irresistible smell of something ticking away slowly on the stove, filling the house, just can't be beaten. But one-pot wonders don't always have to be long, slow European-style braises – you only have to go to Malaysia, Thailand or Vietnam and walk the streets lined with stalls to see the huge variety of food that can be cooked in just a single pot.

For me there are many types of one-pot wonders. There are the heavy, warming braises and casseroles and their simpler cousins, the broths and soups. Then you have the curries from many different cuisines, along with the rice-based dishes where you cook on the stove (like paella and, of course, risotto) or bake in the oven (like pilaf or biryani). The next group would be the stir-fries and then lastly, and the one I often forget, are the oven-tray roast numbers – think beautiful chicken leg quarters on a bed of thinly cut potatoes topped with broccoli and tomatoes, the various ingredients added to the oven at different times and the whole lot served on the tray in the middle of the table for everyone to help themselves. Delicious.

I guess these days one-pot cooking fits with our busier, time-poor lifestyles but I think one of the main reasons for its rising popularity is the simple fact that there is bugger-all washing up to do. As a kid who had to wash up and now a professional cook who gets through a lot of dishes, I can definitely see the appeal.

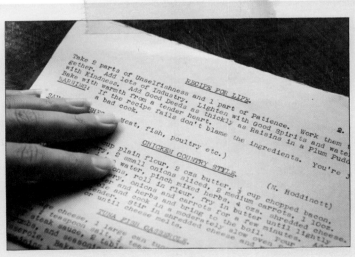

Take 2 parts of Unselfishness and 1 part of Patience. Work them together. Add lots of Industry. Lighten with Good Spirits and water
with Kindness. Add Good Deeds as thickly as Raisins in a Plum Pudd
Bake with warmth from a tender heart.
WARNING: If the recipe fails don't blame the ingredients. You're j
a bad cook.

RECIPE FOR LIFE.

2.

SAU

SHE

meat, fish, poultry etc.)

(N. Hoddinott)

CHICKEN COUNTRY STYLE.

up plain flour. 2 ozs butter. ½ cup chopped bacon.
ry. 2 small onions sliced. 2 medium carrots. 1 10oz.
water, pinch mixed herbs. 4 ozs. shredded cheese.
ons, roll in flour, fry in butter until lightly
ery, onions and carrots and cook for a few minutes.
er and herbs and bring to the boil. Pour
le and cook in a moderately slow oven
nder. Stir in shredded cheese and
or until cheese melts.

TUNA FISH CASSEROLE.

cheese, 1 large can tu
teaspoon salt, ½ tea
steak sauce, 2 tabl
rbs, and seasoning
serole. Bake

Shredded chicken pasta soup

SERVES 4

MRS Perfect for a winter's day; when someone asks me to make a chicken broth this is the recipe I turn to.

1 tablespoon extra-virgin olive oil

500 g (1 lb 2 oz) free-range boneless, skinless chicken thighs

1 leek, white and light green part only, halved lengthways and sliced

500 ml (17 fl oz/2 cups) chicken or vegetable stock

2 × 7 cm (2¾ in) pieces kombu (optional)

80 g (2¾ oz/ ½ cup) soup pasta (such as risoni or mini macaroni)

zest and juice of 1 lemon, plus lemon wedges, to garnish

1 bunch bok choy (pak choy), leaves separated

parsley sprigs, to garnish

Heat the oil in a large saucepan over a medium heat, add the chicken thighs and brown on all sides, then add the leek and sauté for 2 minutes. Pour over the stock and 1 litre (34 fl oz/4 cups) water, add the kombu, if using, and bring to the boil. Reduce the heat to low, cover with a lid and leave to simmer until the chicken is cooked through, about 12 minutes.

Remove the chicken from the pot and shred into pieces using two forks. Set aside.

Meanwhile, add the pasta to the broth, cover with a lid and simmer for a further 10 minutes, until the pasta is cooked through, then add the shredded chicken, lemon juice and zest and bok choy and cook for a further 2 minutes. Spoon into bowls and serve garnished with parsley sprigs.

Risotto

Mum's version

SERVES 4

MRS I learned to cook risotto from Jamie Oliver when I worked with him back in the The Naked Chef era when he was the consulting chef at a private member's club in Knightsbridge, London, I was working at. While my method has changed a bit since then, I still use Jamie's rice measurement, which was a handful of rice per person plus one for the pot, and it has never failed me (though I'm giving you more exact measurements here just in case!). I'm not sure where this came from, but Jay loves to splash balsamic vinegar on his risotto before he eats it and now we all do.

1.25 litres (42 fl oz/5 cups) chicken or vegetable stock

2 tablespoons extra-virgin olive oil

200 g (7 oz) broccoli, cut into florets and stem reserved and diced

1 celery stalk, diced

4 free-range bacon rashers, rind removed and cut into 2 cm (¾ in) pieces

350 g (12½ oz/1⅔ cups) risotto rice (we use carnaroli)

25 g (1 oz) salted butter

50 g (1¾ oz/ ½ cup) parmesan cheese, grated plus extra for serving

salt flakes

balsamic vinegar, to serve

Heat the stock in a saucepan until simmering.

Heat the olive oil in a large saucepan over a medium heat, add the diced broccoli stem, celery and bacon and sauté for 2–3 minutes, or until the bacon is cooked. Add the rice and cook for a further 2 minutes, stirring to coat the grains evenly with the oil.

Spoon a ladleful of the hot stock into the pan and cook, stirring, until absorbed. Continue to cook, stirring regularly and adding a ladleful of the stock at a time, for about 20 minutes, or until all the stock has been absorbed and the rice is soft and moist (if you need to add more liquid you can use hot water from the kettle).

Add the broccoli florets to the pan together with the final ladleful of stock and cook for a further 2 minutes, then remove from the heat. Add the butter and parmesan to the pan, cover and leave to sit for 2 minutes, then remove the lid and give everything a stir. Season the risotto with salt to taste and spoon into bowls, scattering over some more grated parmesan and splashing over a little balsamic vinegar if you like. Serve.

Risotto

Dad's version

SERVES 4

MR Well I learned to cook risotto properly by myself, so there you go Jamie bloody Oliver. I was originally taught to make risotto par-cooked then chill, then re-cook later to order. But after watching Italians cook risotto I came to this way because, well, because Italians can't make risotto.

2 shallots, trimmed (reserving these for the stock, see below) and diced

2 garlic cloves, finely sliced

3 tablespoons extra-virgin olive oil

125 g (4½ oz/ ½ cup) salted butter

440 g (15½ oz/2 cups) risotto rice

250 ml (8½ fl oz/1 cup) white wine

1.3 litres (44 fl oz) Corn stock (see below) or vegetable stock

1 tablespoon rosemary, finely chopped

100 g (3½ oz/ 1 cup) freshly grated parmesan cheese, plus extra to serve

salt flakes and freshly ground black pepper

balsamic vinegar, to serve

CORN STOCK (OPTIONAL)

2 corn cobs, husks removed

1 bunch fresh herbs

piece of parmesan rind

shallot trimmings (see above)

3 garlic cloves

To make the corn stock, add the corn cobs, herbs, parmesan rind, shallot trimmings, garlic and 1.5 litres (51 fl oz/6 cups) water to a large saucepan and bring to the boil. Reduce the heat and simmer for 20 minutes. Take the corn cobs out of the water, slice off and reserve the kernels, then return the cobs to the pan and keep over a low heat.

In a heavy-based frying pan over a medium heat, sauté the shallot and garlic in the oil for 3 minutes, until soft but not coloured. Add the butter and rice and cook for 5 minutes, shaking the pan to move everything around, until the rice is translucent. Increase the heat to high, add the wine and leave it for 4–6 minutes to bubble away and evaporate completely, shaking the pan during this time but NOT stirring it with a spoon. Now start adding the stock a ladleful at a time, making sure all the stock has been absorbed before adding the next ladleful and shaking the pan from side to side as you go so the rice moves around the pan in waves, for 18 minutes or until the rice is glossy, soft and cooked through and the risotto is not too thick but still slightly runny.

Remove the pan from the heat, stir in the rosemary, parmesan and reserved corn kernels and season with salt and pepper. Ladle the risotto onto serving plates, sprinkle over a little more parmesan if you like and splash over a little balsamic vinegar. Serve immediately.

TIP *The corn stock here is great for many things like soup and is something I like to whip up whenever we have corn – saving the left-over cobs and throwing them in the pot as above. The stock will keep in an airtight container for up to 5 days in the fridge or 3 months in the freezer.*

Clams with garlic, lemon & parsley

SERVES 2

MR Clams are one of my favourite foods. I love them both cooked and raw, which, so long as they have been purged properly so there is no sand in them, is a bit like eating an oyster. I have had the pleasure of spending some time at Cloudy Bay Clams in Marlborough, New Zealand, where they produce some of the best and most sustainable aquaculture in the world and it is their clams that I would use for this recipe, though if you can't get your hands on them I suggest you use the best-quality and most sustainable option you can find.

100 ml (3½ fl oz) extra-virgin olive oil

1 garlic bulb, cloves peeled and crushed

2 shallots, diced

1 kg (2 lb 3 oz) diamond shell clams (vongole) large pipis or even mussels, cleaned

100 g (3½ oz) salted butter

2 lemons, cut into quarters, seeds removed and juiced

100 ml (3½ fl oz) verjus or sweet white wine

½ bunch flat-leaf (Italian) parsley, chopped

pinch of cracked black pepper

grilled (broiled) or toasted foccacia slices, to serve

Heat the oil in a small saucepan over a low heat, add the garlic cloves and shallot and cook gently, stirring occasionally, for 5–7 minutes until golden.

Set a large saucepan over a high heat and leave for 1 minute, then add the garlic and shallot mixture, clams, butter, lemons quarters and juice. Cook, stirring, for 30 seconds, then pour over the verjus, cover with a lid and leave for 5–7 minutes, or until the clams have opened.

Remove the pan from the heat and scatter over the parsley and cracked black pepper. Spoon the clams into a serving dish or individual bowls along with the cooking liquor, discarding any shells that haven't opened, and serve with grilled or toasted focaccia alongside a finger bowl of warm lemon water and an empty bowl for the clam shells.

Shakshuka

SERVES 4

> **MRS** This is a flavoursome Middle Eastern dish of baked eggs with the types of spices used varying depending on the country of origin (so feel free to experiment with these to suit your own tastes). There's something very soothing about dipping toasted bread into a dish of this rich, egg-laced tomato-ey stew, though if you like things hot try adding a good pinch of cayenne pepper along with the spices to give it a bit of a kick.

1 tablespoon extra-virgin olive oil

2 red onions, thinly sliced

1 long sweet yellow capsicum (bell pepper), thinly sliced

2 teaspoons ground cumin

2 teaspoons ground coriander

1 teaspoon sweet paprika

2 garlic cloves, thinly sliced

700 g (1 lb 9 oz) tomato passata (puréed tomatoes)

1 teaspoon apple-cider vinegar

salt flakes and freshly ground black pepper

4 free-range eggs

1 handful parsley, leaves only, chopped

1 tablespoon dukkah

1 teaspoon sumac

toasted pide (Turkish bread), to serve

Heat the olive oil in a large frying pan with a lid over a medium heat, add the onions, capsicum and spices and sauté for 2–3 minutes until the onion has softened. Add the garlic and cook, stirring, for a further 30 seconds until the onion is soft and translucent, being careful not to let the spices catch and burn on the bottom of the pan and adding a splash of water if necessary as you go. Pour over the passata, add the apple-cider vinegar and a good pinch of salt and pepper and cook over a low heat for 10–15 minutes until reduced to a thick sauce. Taste and adjust the seasoning if required.

Make four little wells in the sauce with a spoon and crack the eggs into them. Cover the pan with the lid and cook for 5–6 minutes, until the whites are set but the yolks are still soft and runny (for hard yolks cook for 2–3 minutes longer).

Remove the pan from the heat and scatter over the chopped parsley, dukkah and sumac. Serve in the middle of the table with toasted pide for dipping.

Dad's curry

SERVES 4

MR I love a good curry and this one's a cracker. If available, I make it with goat meat as I love its delicate flavour and the way that it soaks up the aromatics of the spices. The longer you leave the meat to marinate, the softer and more flavoursome the curry will be. Note: this is not for chilli cravens.

1 kg (2 lb 3 oz) diced goat or beef

3 tablespoons mustard oil

1 tablespoon kashmiri chilli powder

1 tablespoon ground turmeric

1 tablespoon salt flakes

3 tablespoons non-GMO vegetable oil

2 white onions, sliced

2 garlic cloves, sliced

1½ tablespoons grated fresh ginger

3 tablespoons sugar

1 tablespoon ground cumin

1 tablespoon ground coriander

1 × 400 g (14 oz) tin chopped tomatoes

3 tablespoons malt vinegar

TO SERVE

grilled Flatbreads (page 64)

Cucumber yoghurt (page 40)

salted red onion (see Tip)

Add the meat, mustard oil, chilli powder, turmeric and salt to a bowl and mix everything together well. Cover with a plate, transfer to the refrigerator and leave to marinate for at least 1 hour, or overnight for best results.

Preheat the oven to 170°C (340°F/Gas 3½).

Heat the vegetable oil in a flameproof casserole over a high heat, add the marinated meat and seal briefly on all sides. Remove from the pan with a slotted spoon and set aside.

Add the onion, garlic and ginger to the pan, reduce the heat to medium and sauté for 3–6 minutes until softened. Add the sugar and remaining spices and cook, stirring, for 1 minute then return the sealed meat to the pan together with the chopped tomatoes, 400 ml (13½ fl oz) water and vinegar. Bring to the boil, cover with a lid and transfer to the oven. Leave to cook for 2–3 hours, or until the meat is tender and has started to fall apart.

Serve with grilled flatbreads, cucumber yoghurt and salted red onion (see Tip).

TIP *To make a salted red onion accompaniment, cut 1 red onion in half lengthways and slice into half-moons. Add to a bowl with a large pinch of salt and a pinch of kashmiri chilli powder and mix together well.*

Nanny Carol's one-pot beef casserole

SERVES 4

> **MR** Nanny Carol's my Mum and she's the best one ever – there's nothing like being back in Yorkshire on a cold winter's night with this casserole cooking away in her old Le Creuset pot. That said, she can keep her bloody dumplings …

3 tablespoons extra-virgin olive oil

1 large white onion, diced

500 g (1 lb 2 oz) gravy beef, diced (osso bucco off the bone)

1 beef kidney, peeled, inner removed and diced

2 carrots, diced

1 wedge of small swede (rutabaga), diced

1 celery stalk, diced

1 large potato, diced

1 tablespoon dried lentils

1 tablespoon split peas

1 tablespoon pearl barley

1 tablespoon worcestershire sauce or yorkshire relish

1 litre (34 fl oz/4 cups) beef stock or water (it's my Mum's recipe but I'd use good old water)

salt flakes and freshly ground black pepper

DUMPLINGS (OPTIONAL)

100 g (3½ oz) beef suet

100 g (3½ oz/ ⅔ cup) self-raising flour

pinch of salt flakes

If you're making the dumplings, mix all the ingredients together in a bowl to form a firm dough, then divide the mixture into eight and roll into balls. Set aside.

Heat the oil in a large casserole over a medium heat. Add the onion and fry for 4–5 minutes until golden, then add the diced beef and kidney and brown all over. Add the carrot, swede, celery and potato and sauté for 5 minutes until softened, then stir in the lentils, split peas, pearl barley and worcestershire sauce and pour over the stock or water. Bring to the boil, then reduce the heat to a simmer and cook, covered, for 1½ hours.

Remove the lid, add the dumplings to the casserole, if using, and simmer for a further 20 minutes, turning the dumplings every 5 minutes or so, until the meat is nice and tender, the gravy thickened and reduced, and the dumplings cooked (you can add more stock/boiling water if required depending on the thickness of gravy you prefer). Season to taste, then serve.

Baked veggies & haloumi

SERVES 4 PLUS LEFTOVERS

> **MRS** We love this as there's very minimal prep involved but it tastes delicious. Below is a guide for vegetables and amounts but you can really use whatever veggies you already have at home that roast well and fill up your baking tray. I like to make sure there is a variety of colour and that the veggies are all cut into roughly the same size chunks so that they will cook evenly. Left-over veggies could be used in the Frittata muffins (page 48) or Bibimbap (page 148).

3 all-purpose potatoes

1 sweet potato

¼ jap or kent pumpkin (squash)

¼ cauliflower, outer leaves removed

1 carrot

1 zucchini (courgette)

3 tablespoons extra-virgin olive oil

1 teaspoon salt flakes

2 garlic cloves, skin on and crushed

1 rosemary sprig

250 g (9 oz) haloumi, cut into thin slices

TO SERVE (OPTIONAL)

Vampire pesto (page 202)

Sugo (page 160)

Preheat the oven to 180°C (350°F/Gas 4).

Cut all the veggies into rough 3–5 cm (1¼–2 in) chunks, then throw them into a large ovenproof dish. Drizzle over the oil, add the salt, garlic and rosemary and mix everything together with your hands to ensure the veggies are evenly coated in the oil.

Transfer the dish to the oven and bake for 40 minutes, then lay the haloumi strips over the veggies and bake for a further 15–20 minutes, or until the vegetables are cooked through and the haloumi is crisp and golden. Divide among plates and serve as is or drizzled with Vampire pesto (page 202) or Sugo (page 160).

Avi's Mauritian bean soup

SERVES 2

MRS When Finn started school last year it was really lovely to become part of the school community. We had an awesome group of prep parents that love picnics in the park, dinners out and limoncello (you know who you are!) and who have become close friends. Avi and Kate are parents from the class and this simple, quick-to-make soup is a regular on their dinner table.

3 tablespoons non-GMO vegetable oil

1 white onion, finely diced

2 garlic cloves, crushed

2 cm (¾ in) piece fresh ginger, finely grated

1 teaspoon salt flakes

¼ teaspoon dried thyme

1 teaspoon ground cumin

3 tomatoes, roughly chopped

1 × 400 g (14 oz) tin butterbeans, black-eyed peas or red kidney beans, drained

1 handful English spinach, silverbeet (Swiss chard) or tuscan kale, chopped

1 small red chilli, chopped (optional)

¼ bunch of coriander (cilantro), chopped, plus extra to garnish

Heat the oil in a frying pan over a low heat, add the onion, garlic and ginger and sauté for 5 minutes until softened and fragrant. Add the salt, thyme, cumin and tomatoes, cover with a lid and cook for about 10 minutes, or until the tomatoes are soft. Stir in the beans and 250 ml (8½ fl oz) water and bring to the boil, then reduce the heat to low and simmer gently for 10 minutes.

Add the spinach and red chilli, if using, and cook for a further 2–3 minutes, then remove from the heat and stir through the coriander. Divide between bowls, scatter over a little extra coriander to finish and serve.

A LITTLE NOTE FROM AVI
As well as being served as a soup, this can also be enjoyed with rice, cucumber salad and sautéed bitter gourd or chokos (chayotes) as sides, which is how we would eat it back home. Generally we would use dried beans soaked overnight and cooked in the pressure cooker but I have substituted tinned here for ease.

Jo's tuna pasta

SERVES 4

> **MR** I don't know what it is about tinned tuna but I think it's rank (that's Yorkshire for disgusting). Having said that, this pasta dish is delicious and could turn me. The recipe comes from Jo Courtney – friend, farmer and one half of Bridge Farm Organics with her husband, Trevor. They grow amazing asparagus and rhubarb that I have been using for years. The original recipe comes from a lady, Mrs Lorenzetto, who used to look after Jo when she was a young pup.

500 g (1 lb 2 oz) penne, fusilli or casarecce

100 ml (3½ fl oz) extra-virgin olive oil

1 white onion, finely diced

3 tablespoons tomato paste (concentrated purée)

2 tablespoons vincotto or balsamic vinegar

45 g (1½ oz) good-quality tinned anchovies in oil

185 g (6½ oz) good-quality tinned tuna in oil

freshly grated parmesan cheese, to serve

Bring a large saucepan of salted water to the boil, add the pasta and cook according to the packet instructions until al dente. Drain the pasta over a bowl, reserving the cooking water, return to the pan and set aside.

Heat the oil in a separate saucepan over a medium heat, add the onion and cook for 3–5 minutes until softened. Add the tomato paste, vincotto and anchovies together with the oil from the tuna tin, reduce the heat to low and cook gently for 5–8 minutes, until the onions are nicely caramelised. Add the tuna and a few splashes of the reserved pasta cooking water, increase the heat to high and cook for 10–15 minutes, adding extra splashes of the pasta water as you go, until the sauce has a thin paste-like consistency.

Tip the sauce into the pan with the pasta and toss together thoroughly to coat. Divide among bowls and scatter over lots of grated parmesan. Serve.

Me Mum's sausage hotpot with baked potatoes

SERVES 4

MR This sausage hotpot is based off the one my Mum made when I was a kid and it's perfect with a baked potato. That said, she used to use Heinz baked beans instead of white beans. Sharlee doesn't like using the microwave (something about the radiation) but I ... well, baked potatoes take a long time to cook and following the method below will more than halve your cooking time. Just don't tell Sharlee I told you.

2 tablespoons non-GMO vegetable oil

5 pork or beef sausages, each cut into four even-sized pieces

1 celery stalk, diced

1 carrots, diced

1 white onion, diced

2 tablespoons tomato paste (concentrated purée)

2 tablespoons worcestershire sauce

1 × 400 g (14 oz) tin cannellini (lima) beans or butterbeans, drained

BAKED POTATOES

4 medium–large potatoes

butter, to serve

100 g (3½ oz) cheddar, grated

Preheat the oven to 220°C (430°F/Gas 7).

Heat the oil in a large saucepan over a high heat, add the sausages and brown all over, then remove the sausages from the pan. Lower the heat to medium, add the vegetables to the pan and cook for 3–4 minutes until softened. Stir in the tomato paste and cook for a further 2–3 minutes, then add the sausage pieces, 200 ml (7 fl oz) water, worcestershire sauce and beans and bring to the boil. Reduce to a simmer and cook for 12–15 minutes, until the sausages are cooked through and the sauce is nice and thick.

Meanwhile, bake the potatoes. Prick the potatoes all over with a fork, then transfer to a microwave and cook on high for 8 minutes. Remove from the microwave, transfer to the oven and cook for a further 8 minutes. Alternatively, cook in the oven only for 35–45 minutes).

To serve, cut open the baked potatoes and add butter, then spoon over the hotpot and scatter over the cheddar to finish.

Corned beef with parsley sauce

SERVES 4

A staple of both of ours growing up, this is still a favourite in our household during the colder months. Here is our go-to recipe, plus some delicious things that we do with the leftovers.

> **MR** This is one of those dishes that I pop straight into the slow cooker before heading to work in the morning and is ready around 4 pm. If I'm eating this hot, it has to be with parsley sauce but I do love it cold on a sandwich too.

1 × 600 g (1 lb 5 oz) corned beef cut (such as brisket, silverside or girello)

½ teaspoon black peppercorns

1 bay leaf

boiled carrots, potatoes and green beans, to serve

piccalilli, to serve

PARSLEY SAUCE

50 g (1¾ oz) salted butter

50 g (1¾ oz/ ⅓ cup) plain (all-purpose) flour

500 ml (17 fl oz/2 cups) milk, plus extra if necessary

30 g (1 oz/ ½ cup) flat-leaf (Italian) parsley, chopped

Place the corned beef, peppercorns and bay leaf in a stockpot and pour over 2½ litres (85 fl oz/10 cups) water. Bring to the boil, reduce to a simmer and cook over a medium heat for 2½–3½ hours, until tender.

Meanwhile, make the parsley sauce. In a small saucepan over a medium heat, melt the butter, then add the flour and beat together to form a paste (roux). Stirring all the while, add the milk little by little until it has all been incorporated to form a smooth white sauce. Stir in the chopped parsley and keep warm.

Drain the corned beef and cut into thick slices. Divide among plates and serve with the parsley sauce, boiled carrots, potatoes and green beans and a generous dollop or two of piccalilli.

Reuben sandwich

MAKES 2

> **MR** I'm not here to debate the history of this sandwich, just to tell you that it's delicious. This one that comes and goes on the menu at Pope Joan is a winner.

4 slices cornbread or rye bread

2 tablespoons Russian mayo (see below)

4–6 slices Corned beef (page 188)

4 slices smoked mozzarella, emmental or cheddar

2 tablespoons pickled red cabbage or sauerkraut

RUSSIAN MAYO

80 g (2¾ oz) Mayo (page 245)

pinch of cayenne pepper

small pinch of smoked paprika

¼ teaspoon horseradish paste, horseradish cream or mustard (optional)

juice of ¼ lemon

pinch of salt flakes

For the Russian mayo, put all the ingredients in a bowl and mix together well.

Lay the bread slices down on a board and spread generously with the mayo like butter. Top two of the slices with the corned beef slices, cheese and pickled cabbage, then lay over the remaining bread slices and sandwich together. Transfer the sandwiches to a toasted sandwich press or a lightly oiled pan and cook for 6–8 minutes until golden and crunchy, pressing down lightly with a spatula and turning halfway through if cooking in the pan. Serve.

Bubble 'n' squeak

MAKES 4

> **MR** There is no dish better for using up leftovers than good old bubble 'n' squeak. It is, after all, usually made with left-over Sunday roast veg, and I remember having many a version as a little one on a Monday. This one makes a great breakfast served with bacon, eggs and beans, or a lovely lunch or dinner with a salad or braised red cabbage and brown sauce.

400 g (14 oz) all-purpose potato, cut into 3 cm (1¼ in) chunks

200 g (7 oz) Corned beef, shredded (page 188)

1 tablespoon wholegrain or dijon mustard

2 tablespoons melted duck fat, pork fat or butter (or olive oil if you want to be healthy)

1 free-range egg, beaten

2 tablespoons chopped parsley, chives or thyme

½ tablespoon sherry vinegar or good white-wine vinegar

plain flour, for dusting

2 tablespoons non-GMO vegetable oil

salt flakes and freshly ground black pepper

Add the potatoes to a large saucepan and cover with water. Bring to the boil and cook for 15–18 minutes or until the potatoes are soft and can be easily pierced with the point of a sharp knife. Turn off the heat and drain the potatoes, then return them to the pan and leave it on the hot hob to dry out.

Once dry, roughly mash the potatoes in the pan with a masher or fork, then add all the remaining ingredients except the oil and mix together thoroughly. Season to taste. Divide the bubble 'n' squeak mixture into four equal-sized pieces, shape into balls and press down lightly on each to form patties around 10 cm (4 in) in diameter. Dust lightly with flour (or, if you prefer, crumb as per the schnitzel recipe on page 154).

Heat the oil in a large frying pan over a medium heat. Add the bubble 'n' squeak patties to the pan and fry for 2–3 minutes on each side until golden. Serve.

Fried rice

SERVES 4

> **MR** I love fried rice. This is Sharlee's version and if we don't have any left-over corned beef we swap it out for bacon, ham or even salami – whatever we can find in the fridge, really.

2 free-range eggs

2 teaspoons sesame oil

1 tablespoon soy sauce, plus extra to serve

1½ tablespoons extra-virgin olive oil

1 carrot, cut into thin rounds

2 spring onions (scallions), finely sliced

3 cm (1¼ in) piece fresh ginger, grated

740 g (1 lb 10 oz/4 cups) cooked rice (white or brown)

80 g (2¾ oz/ ½ cup) frozen peas

1 large handful corned beef, chopped or shredded

kecap manis and chilli sauce, to serve

Whisk the eggs together with 1 teaspoon of the sesame oil in a bowl. Mix the soy sauce together with the remaining sesame oil in a separate small bowl.

Heat ½ tablespoon olive oil in a large frying pan or wok over a medium heat. Pour the eggs into the pan and cook like a pancake, until set and golden. Remove from the pan and cut into thin strips. Set aside.

Heat the remaining olive oil in the same pan over a high heat, add the carrot, spring onion and ginger and stir-fry for 2–3 minutes. Add the cooked rice and frozen peas and stir-fry for another 3–4 minutes, then stir through the corned beef and continue to cook until heated through. Pour the soy sauce mixture into the pan and toss through, then remove from the heat and divide among bowls. Serve with kecap manis, chilli sauce and extra soy sauce on the table for everyone to help themselves.

When *When* Mum's Away
When Dad's Away

MRS One of the tough things about the hospitality industry and having a chef in your family is that there are bound to be nights where they are at work cooking. Luckily for us Pope Joan is only open three nights a week so this doesn't happen so much anymore, but every week there are a couple of nights when Matt is unfortunately not home for dinner.

When this happens, we still have the same routine and sit down to eat at the same time, but we probably do things a bit differently in the kitchen. For me, the key is to fall back on recipes that don't require long periods of cooking or preparation. Recipes the boys and I love to eat and Matt is not a fan of make the cut here along with other dinner favourites like Mum's risotto (page 172) or Bacon & egg pie (page 134). You won't find me cooking big slabs of meat, so it tends to be veggie-focused dishes that are nice and versatile so that I can switch things up a bit if necessary – maybe putting that pesto on the side of a plate of veggies or mixing it with ricotta and stuffing it into sweet yellow capsicums, for example, or spreading an eggplant sugo over a pizza or using it to stuff chicken breasts.

MR It is quite rare for Sharlee to be away from us at all, let alone for a night or a long weekend but every now and then the boys and I get to go wild. I will admit it, when this happens I spoil them rotten – we go get ice cream and eat chocolate, we have a movie fiesta and watch 2–3 episodes of Star Wars, or go shopping for toys and head to the park with the kite or cricket kit. When it comes to the food I cook things that Sharlee doesn't like but I love, like lamb and offal. It is sometimes a hit with the boys and sometimes not. We have had black pudding many times, which they love, but not haggis, as Finn thinks it's, 'too spicy Dad'. I remember like yesterday the time I was boiling tripe to make an Italian-style tomato and tripe braise and the boys came into the kitchen asking what that 'horrible stink' was. Later that night as we sat down to the 'curly tripe pasta', which they devoured two bowls of each, Finn's comment was, 'We love that curly pasta Dad – can we have it again with Mum?' Erm, no!

Pan-fried liver with onion gravy

SERVES 3

> **MR** This is all about proper mash and good onion gravy – the one here's vegetarian and really delicious, a little take on a French onion soup recipe from my first book. If I'm honest the kids are 50/50 on the liver. Sometimes they like it, sometimes they don't, and when the Mrs is at home I replace it with sausages.

4 × 100 g (3½ oz) thin slices fresh calve's liver, trimmed

100 ml (3½ fl oz) milk

50 g (1¾ oz/ ⅓ cup) plain (all-purpose) flour

1 tablespoon extra-virgin olive oil

ONION GRAVY

60 ml (2 fl oz/ ¼ cup) extra-virgin olive oil

50 g (1¾ oz) unsalted butter

3 large white onions, finely sliced

3 large garlic cloves, finely sliced

1 teaspoon thyme leaves

1 tablespoon Vegemite or other yeast extract spread

1 tablespoon quince jelly, or redcurrant jelly

1 tablespoon cornflour (cornstarch)

3 tablespoons good quality apple-cider vinegar

150 ml (5 fl oz) white verjus or white wine

Proper mash, to serve (page 247)

Put the liver in a bowl and pour over the milk. Cover and transfer to the fridge. Leave to soak for at least 2–3 hours, ideally overnight, removing from the fridge ten minutes before you begin cooking to warm to room temperature.

To make the gravy, heat the oil and butter in a large heavy-based saucepan over a high heat. Once the butter is foaming, add the onions, garlic and thyme, reduce the heat to low and cook for about 20 minutes, or until the onion and garlic are caramelised. Stir in the Vegemite and quince jelly and cook for another 5 minutes, then add the cornflour and stir. Pour over the vinegar and verjus or wine and stir to deglaze the the pan. Add 1 litre (34 fl oz/4 cups) water to the pan and bring to the boil, then reduce to a simmer and cook for a further 12–15 minutes, to a lovely thick gravy consistency. Keep warm.

For the mash, see page 247. Once made, set it aside.

Remove the soaked liver pieces from the milk and pat dry on paper towel, then dust with the flour. Heat the oil in a large frying pan over a medium heat, add the liver and cook for 2 minutes on each side, then pour over the warm onion gravy and cook for a further 2–3 minutes, until the liver is nicely pink on the inside. Divide among plates and serve with the mash.

Cowboy dinner – homemade kipfler chips, sausage, eggs, baked beans & toast

SERVES 3

MR My uncle Andrew, my Mum's little brother, had Down's syndrome and his favourite meal was called cowboy dinner – I guess because he loved to dress up as a cowboy (he also loved to play cricket in the full English cricket gear). Keeping his spirit alive, we now have it when Mum's away.

9 kipfler (fingerling) potatoes, cut into halves or quarters lengthways

2 tablespoons beef dripping, duck fat, ghee or olive oil

3 free-range pork sausages

3 free-range eggs

420 g (15 oz) baked beans (tinned or homemade, see page 244)

buttered wholegrain toast and tomato sauce (ketchup), to serve

Preheat the oven to 200°C (400°F/Gas 6).

Place the potato quarters in a saucepan and rinse with cold water. Drain. Fill the pan with water again until the potatoes are just covered, then transfer to the stove top, bring to the boil and cook for 4 minutes.

Strain the par-cooked potatoes, transfer to a baking tray with your fat of choice and mix together well. Bake for 35 minutes, or until golden and crunchy.

While the chips are cooking, get everything else ready. Seal the sausages in a frying pan. Remove from the pan and place in an ovenproof dish, transfer to the oven and cook for 8 minutes until nicely golden. Fry the eggs to your liking and warm the baked beans in another saucepan over a low heat.

Divide everything among plates and serve with buttered wholegrain toast and lots of tomato sauce. Boom ... cowboy dinner.

Dad's burgers

MAKES 8 BURGERS

> **MR** Everybody loves a good burger, don't they? But with so many burger joints open around the place, 'Why on earth would you make them at home?' I hear you ask. Easy: they are fun to make and cook and can be just as good as the ones down the road.

700 g (1 lb 9 oz) minced (ground) veal

300 g (10½ oz) free-range minced (ground) pork

2 tablespoons capers, rinsed and chopped

salt flakes and freshly ground black pepper to taste

TO SERVE

soft burger buns, halved

cheddar slices

pickled beetroot (beet) slices, preferably home-made (though tinned is fine)

bread and butter pickles or sliced large pickled cucumbers

tomato sauce (ketchup)

hot English mustard

iceberg lettuce leaves

Put all the ingredients in a large mixing bowl and mix vigorously, slapping the meat around with your hands, so that everything is really well combined. Divide the mixture into eight equal-sized pieces and roll into balls, then transfer any that you don't need to the freezer in a suitable container for later.

Heat a barbecue or large frying pan over a high heat. Add the meatballs to the pan in batches, flattening them down with a spatula to shape into patties and cook for 4–5 minutes per side or until done to your liking. Set aside and keep warm as you cook the rest.

To serve, pile the patties into buns and top with cheddar, beetroot, bread and butter pickles, tomato sauce, mustard and iceberg lettuce leaves (or just the tomato sauce if you're like the boys). Yum.

Vampire pesto pasta

SERVES 4

> **MRS** Matt's not too keen on pesto (it's the pine nuts he doesn't like) but this is one of my go-to dinner dishes for when there's not much time to cook. This garlic-free version is good for both vampires and the boys, who – despite saying they don't like green stuff on their plates – for some reason devour pesto pasta.

300 g (10½ oz) linguine

½ broccoli head, cut into florets (optional)

1 handful green beans, trimmed (optional)

freshly grated parmesan cheese, to serve

Vampire pesto (see below) or 60 g (2 oz) pre-made pesto of your choice

VAMPIRE PESTO

3 tablespoons cashew nuts

1 tablespoon pine nuts, lightly toasted

1 bunch basil, leaves only

40 g (1½ oz) parmesan cheese, grated

pinch of salt flakes

squeeze of lemon juice

60 ml (2 fl oz/ ¼ cup) extra-virgin olive oil, plus extra to cover

To make the pesto, blitz all the ingredients together in a food processor to a rough paste. Taste and add more salt or lemon juice if desired.

Cook the pasta in a saucepan of boiling water according to the packet instructions until al dente, adding the broccoli florets and green beans, if using, to the pasta water for the last few minutes. Drain and return to the pan, then toss through half the pesto. Divide among bowls and sprinkle over some grated parmesan to finish.

TIP *Spoon the excess pesto into an airtight container, cover the surface with extra oil and keep in the refrigerator for up to 1 week until needed. At the end of summer I like to scale this recipe up and make it with the last basil of the season, dividing it into portions, freezing it (it'll keep for 6 months) and defrosting as needed.*

Apricot chicken 2017

SERVES 4

> **MRS** I am pretty sure most Australians growing up in the '70s and '80s had apricot chicken and it was certainly a regular in our household … chicken, apricot nectar, French onion soup mix and, voila, it was done. I've gone to the next level with my interpretation of this Aussie classic. The boys love chicken on the bone, so this is a guaranteed winner for dinner. If you are going old school, serve it on a bed of rice sprinkled with parsley, though I like to serve it with a toasted couscous salad bursting with almonds, sunflower seeds and feta (see page 241).

75 g (2¾ oz/ ½ cup) plain (all-purpose) flour

1 teaspoon ground turmeric

2 teaspoons dukkah

8 free-range chicken drumsticks

2 tablespoons extra-virgin olive oil

1 teaspoon Promite or other yeast extract–based spread (optional)

600 ml (20½ fl oz) apricot nectar

¼ cauliflower, cut into small florets

5–6 apricots, halved (fresh or tinned)

1 teaspoon apple-cider vinegar

salt flakes to taste

rice or The Mrs' toasted couscous salad (page 241), to serve

Put the flour and spices in a bowl, add two of the drumsticks and shake to coat. Remove and set aside on a plate, then repeat with the remaining drumsticks.

Heat 1 tablespoon of the olive oil in a large saucepan over a medium heat. Add half the drumsticks and brown all over. Remove from the pan and set aside, then add the rest of the oil and repeat with the remaining drumsticks, setting them aside once browned along with the first batch.

Add the Promite, nectar and 100 ml (3½ fl oz) water to the pan and cook, stirring, for 2–3 minutes, until the Promite has dissolved. Return the drumsticks to the pan and bring to the boil, then reduce the heat to a simmer, cover with a lid and cook for 10 minutes, until the drumsticks are just cooked through. Remove the lid, add the cauliflower, apricots and vinegar and cook, uncovered, for a further 2–3 minutes or until the cauliflower is soft. Season to taste with salt and serve with rice or a toasted couscous salad.

Eggplant, bacon & tomato fusilli

SERVES 4

> **MRS** I love cooking with eggplants in the late summer and early autumn while it's still warm – we grow them in the garden and they provide a nice base for this chunky sauce. The bacon here is optional but it gives everything a lovely salty, smokiness that takes it to the next level.

1 tablespoon extra-virgin olive oil, plus extra if necessary

1 red onion, sliced

1 eggplant, cut into 1 cm (½ in) cubes

1 teaspoon dried oregano

4 free-range bacon rashers, sliced

1 × 400 g (14 oz) tin chopped tomatoes

1 teaspoon apple-cider vinegar

1 tablespoon tomato paste (concentrated purée)

pinch of salt flakes

400 g (14 oz) fusilli pasta

100 g (3½ oz) feta, crumbled

1 handful parsley, roughly chopped (optional)

Heat the olive oil in a large saucepan over a medium heat, add the onion and cook for 1–2 minutes, until slightly softened. Add the eggplant and oregano, toss to coat in the olive oil and cook for 2–3 minutes, adding a splash more oil if the eggplant absorbs it all and the pan is looking dry. Add the bacon and toss to combine, then cook for another 3–4 minutes, until the eggplant is tender. Stir in the tomatoes, vinegar, tomato paste and salt and bring to the boil, then reduce the heat to a simmer and leave to cook for 10–15 minutes, until the sauce has thickened and reduced.

Meanwhile, bring a separate large saucepan of water to the boil, add the fusilli and cook according to the packet instructions. Reserving a small cup of the pasta cooking water, drain the fusilli, then add it to the pan with the eggplant sugo. Toss everything together, adding a splash of the pasta cooking water, then divide among bowls. Scatter over the feta and parsley and serve.

When the Kids are Away

MR Life really is about different moments in time. There was a time when every night for us was a date night and we would spend our evenings heading out to restaurants for dinner or enjoying romantic nights in with candles and all that soppy stuff (and that was just me doing that, Sharlee is way tougher). Then kids came along … and now the set-up for a night off is to get the hell out of the house as quickly as possible leaving the little darlings with the sitter (thanks Effie!), to enjoy dinner and then to race back to make sure that everyone's ok and that the house hasn't burnt down. Times have changed.

It is lovely, though, when you do get the house to yourself, kids or not, to actually be able to take the time to sit down, share a meal and talk to one another. This is why I think food and the table we eat it on plays such an important role in all our lives (well, it does for us), helping provide that shared point of connection. So here are a couple of menus that we have enjoyed together in the past – full of simple, easy things that we both love to eat and share together indoors and out, and a little more grown up than what we eat every day.

Chilli & lime squid

SERVES 2

> **MR** A favourite on the Pope Joan night-time Summer Camp Cookout sessions, this is a really simple and lovely dish.

zest and juice of 1 lime

1 teaspoon chilli flakes

2 tablespoons salt flakes

½ teaspoon sugar

1 × 200–250 g (7–9 oz) squid tube, cleaned and cut in half

2 tablespoons extra-virgin olive oil

1 large Lebanese (short) cucumber, halved, seeds removed and cut into four

30 g (1 oz/ ½ cup) flat-leaf (Italian) parsley, leaves only

30 g (1 oz/ ½ cup) dill, fronds torn

2 tablespoons sour cream

Put the lime zest, chilli flakes, salt and sugar in a bowl and mix together well.

Brush the squid halves with the olive oil and sprinkle generously with the lime salt, then transfer to a hot barbecue or chargrill pan and cook for 3–4 minutes on each side. Using tongs, remove the squid from the heat and cut into strips, then return to the barbecue or pan and cook for a further 3–4 minutes, until nicely charred all over.

Transfer the squid strips to a bowl and sprinkle again with the lime salt, then pour over the lime juice and mix well. Add the cucumber, herbs and another sprinkle of lime salt and mix again. To serve, spread the sour cream over a platter, then pile over the squid mixture.

Pictured on page 210

Smoked tomato romesco mussels

SERVES 2

> **MR** A play on simple mussels in tomato, the smoked tomato romesco here is an adaptation of a recipe from my first book and can be made with regular or smoked tomatoes.

3 tablespoons extra-virgin olive oil

1 kg (2 lb 3 oz) mussels, scrubbed and beards removed

1 bread loaf, sliced and warmed

SMOKED TOMATO ROMESCO

150 g (5½ oz) Smoked tomatoes (page 213) or roma (plum) tomatoes

50 g (1¾ oz) jarred roasted red capsicum (bell pepper)

50 ml (1¾ fl oz) extra-virgin olive oil

¼ teaspoon fennel seeds

¼ teaspoon coriander seeds

¼ teaspoon nigella seeds

¼ teaspoon cumin seeds

¼ teaspoon sumac

¼ teaspoon smoked paprika

2 teaspoons cabernet vinegar or good red-wine vinegar

1 teaspoon quince paste or honey

salt flakes and freshly ground black pepper

To make the smoked tomato romesco, place everything into a food processor and blend together to a rough, slightly chunky paste. Set aside until needed.

Heat a large saucepan over a high heat. Add the olive oil then the mussels to the pan and cook, stirring, for 2 minutes, then pour over the romesco, cover with the lid and cook for a further 8 minutes, or until the mussels have opened. Carefully spoon the mussels into a large serving bowl together with the cooking liquor, discarding any shells that haven't opened, and serve with the chargrilled bread alongside a finger bowl of warm lemon water and an empty bowl for the mussel shells.

Pictured on page 211

Summer crostata

SERVES 8

> **MRS** Taking the time to make this pastry is well worth it and will win you some serious brownie points. I used apricots and nectarines here but you can use any stone fruit you like.

150 g (5½ oz) cold unsalted butter, cut into 1 cm (½ in) cubes

200 g (7 oz/1⅓ cups) plain (all-purpose) flour

100 g (3½ oz) sour cream

400 g (14 oz) mixed berries (such as raspberries, blueberries and strawberries)

100 g (3½ oz) apricots, quartered and stones removed

100 g (3½ oz) nectarines, quartered and stones removed

50 g (1¾ oz) raw (demerara) sugar

1 free-range egg yolk, beaten

vanilla ice cream or softly whipped cream, to serve

Preheat the oven to 180°C (350°F/Gas 4) and insert a baking tray to heat up.

Add the butter and flour to a food processor and pulse together until the mixture resembles fine breadcrumbs, then pour over the sour cream and pulse again to form a soft dough.

Transfer the dough to the centre of a 30 cm (12 in) square of baking paper and shape it into a rough circle, then wrap it tightly and transfer to the fridge to chill for 15 minutes.

Combine the berries, apricot and nectarine slices in a large bowl. Add the sugar and gently mix together. Set aside.

Remove the dough from the fridge and roll it out into a rough circle approximately 5 mm (¼ in) thick. Remove the top sheet of baking paper and arrange the fruit in the centre of the pastry circle, being sure to leave a 4–5 cm (1½–2 in) border around the outside.

Fold the sides of the pastry over to enclose the fruit, repairing any breaks in the pastry as necessary, then transfer the crostata, still on the baking paper, to the hot baking tray. Brush the pastry with the beaten egg yolk and bake for 60 minutes, or until the pastry is golden and flaky and the fruit is warmed through.

Leave to cool slightly, then cut into slices and serve warm with ice cream or cream.

Scallops with miso butter

SERVES 2

> **MR** This recipe makes plenty of the miso butter, which alone is to die for. I store the extra in the fridge (where it will keep for about 3 months) and use it to top grilled steak, fish and veg. Though with seafood – particularly scallops – it's truly amazing.

250 g (9 oz) unsalted butter, diced and softened

3 tablespoons red or yellow miso paste

juice of 1 lemon

12 scallops on their shells, cleaned

Add the butter, miso paste and lemon to a bowl and beat together with a fork. Spoon the butter into the centre of a piece of plastic wrap, roll into a sausage and twist the ends to seal. Transfer to the refrigerator to chill and firm.

Once firm, cut thin discs of the butter and lay them over the scallops in the shell. Place the scallops shell down on a hot barbecue or under a grill (broiler) on low heat and cook for 1–2 minutes, or until cooked through. Transfer to a serving platter and eat straight from the shell.

A NOTE ON SALT FROM MATT ...

Not all salt is the same. Because of the varying amounts of these minerals and trace elements, natural salts from different parts of the world taste different. Natural sea salt should have an almost sweet, sea salt tang while salts from lakes or from mines, assuming they have not been overly processed, should have a flavour profile specific to their regions.

As well as flavour, another key characteristic of salt is its texture. There is rock salt (the type that's mined), solar salt crystal (where the salt is evaporated from water, whether lake or sea) and flaked salt. Texturally, with crystal salt, the main difference is the grain size. A larger sized grain like rock or table salt weighs less per spoon than say a fine salt or cooking salt grade. Chefs and cooks (and me) use salt crystals or flaked salt, which weighs even less per spoonful than fine salt. So if you're cooking a recipe from a book, TV or the internet, always use salt flakes. I love using Olsson's Salt, the oldest family-owned salt company in Australia. Their sea salt flakes are brilliant for cooking with and finishing dishes and have a sweet, delicate flavour that is 100 per cent natural. One last thing, my Nan and Mum might as well not add salt. A 'Nan's pinch' as I call it, is about 1 gram, while a chef's pinch is roughly 3–4 grams of salt. That's a big difference, but if you do get scared of oversalting dishes during the cooking process, it's fine to simply add it in at the end (though you could tell my Nan and Mum that for me).

Pictured on page 218

Cashew curry & chilli sambol

SERVES 2

MR For our honeymoon we headed to Sri Lanka, where I have to say the food was quite possibly the best I have ever had. This cashew curry served alongside this delicious sambol was one of many highlights.

160 g (5½ oz/1 cup) raw cashew nuts

½ teaspoon coriander seeds

1 × 2 cm (¾ in) piece cinnamon stick

1 cardamom pod

3 dried curry leaves

¼ teaspoon fennel seeds

¼ teaspoon cumin seeds

3 tablespoons non-GMO vegetable oil

5 fresh curry leaves

1 green chilli, seeded and finely sliced

2 garlic cloves, finely sliced

2 shallots, finely diced

5 baby okra

1 lime leaf

juice of 1 lime

200 ml (7 fl oz) coconut milk

rice and Flatbreads, to serve (page 64)

CHILLI SAMBOL

1 fresh brown coconut, flesh finely grated (or 90 g/3 oz desiccated coconut, soaked in boiling water)

2 shallots, finely sliced

good pinch of salt flakes

2 small bullet chillies, seeded and finely sliced

juice of 2 limes

tiny pinch of chilli powder

To make the chilli sambol, put everything in a bowl and mix together well. Set aside.

Place the cashew nuts in a bowl, cover with boiling water and pour and leave to soak for 30 minutes.

Meanwhile, add the coriander, cinnamon, cardamom, dried curry leaves, fennel seeds and cumin seeds to a blender and blitz together. Set aside.

Heat the oil in a heavy-based saucepan or cast-iron casserole pot over a high heat. Add the fresh curry leaves and the spice mixture and fry for 1–2 minutes until crisp and fragrant, then lower the heat to medium, add the chilli, garlic and shallot and cook, stirring, for 5 minutes until softened. Stir in the okra and lime leaf, then pour over the coconut milk and bring to the boil. Drain the soaked cashew nuts and add them to the pan, then reduce the heat to a simmer and cook for a further 3–4 minutes. Divide between bowls and serve with the sambol, some steamed rice if needed and some Flatbreads (page 64).

Nectarine upside-down cake

SERVES 8

> **MRS** Matt reckons that this is the cake I won him over with, and it's one of my favourite desserts of all time. I learned the original recipe during my time at Ballymaloe Cookery School in Ireland and here I've made it with nectarines, though you could use peaches or plums instead.

125 g (4½ oz/ ½ cup) unsalted butter

125 g (4½ oz) raw (demerara) sugar

1 teaspoon vanilla paste

2 free-range eggs

125 g (4½ oz) self-raising flour

280 g (10 oz) sugar

6 nectarines, halved and stones removed

cream or ice cream, to serve

Preheat the oven to 180°C (350°F/Gas 4).

Beat the butter and raw sugar together in a mixing bowl until light and fluffy. Add the vanilla paste and eggs and whisk until creamy; then stir in the flour and mix well to form a thick batter. Set aside.

Put the sugar and 150 ml (5 fl oz) water in a flameproof casserole dish and cook over a medium–low heat, without stirring, until a golden brown caramel develops (be sure to watch it carefully at this point as you don't want the caramel to burn).

Remove the casserole dish from the heat and carefully drop the nectarine halves into the caramel cut side down in an even layer (this will stop the caramel cooking further). Carefully spoon the batter evenly over the fruit and smooth the top, then place in the oven and bake for 50 minutes, or until the cake comes away from the edges of the dish.

Remove the cake from the oven and leave to rest for 2 minutes, then cover the dish with a serving platter and turn it upside down to invert the cake onto the plate. Rearrange any nectarine pieces that may have got stuck to the pan and serve warm with cream or ice cream. Any leftovers can be stored in an airtight container in the fridge for 3–4 days.

Drinks

MR I'll be honest and you can be Frank, I love a drink. It's the whole socialising, being relaxed thing and, in moderation, it really is quite lovely. Sharlee isn't the biggest drinker – in fact a little sip of mine here and there and the odd aperol spritz, glass of bubbles, G&T or glass of vermentino is really all she'll have. Me on the other hand, well … all of the above and the rest. My Dad used to work for a brewery and then lived above a pub called the Crown and Cushion in Sheffield, owned by his best friend, Alan Jane, and run by his son Robert (who taught me many a valuable lesson about the food and drink industry and life in general). So I guess food, booze and the hospitality industry was always my destiny.

If I was to list my favourite drinks, beer would have to be at the top. That's beer as in the English 'bitter', which is meant to be drunk at cellar temperature, as well as lager, which needs to be served nice and cold as it is here in Australia. Tight second would be wine, with pinot noir and chenin blanc varietals top of the list along with my good friend Mac Forbes' wines from the Yarra Valley. Sake's pretty delicious too, as is the Italian liqueur Varnelli l'Anise Secco. And when it comes to cocktails I'm a big fan of the rum monty – a shot of half dark rum and Amaro Montenegro – but the king for me is the dirty martini.

It's not all booze here though. There's a recipe for a lovely raspberry and lemon verbena cordial here too, along with the hooligans' favourite hot chocolate. So what are you waiting for? Sit down, pour yourself a glass (or mug) and have one on me.

Jimmy's punch #4

SERVES 1

> **MR** Jimmy works for me at Pope Joan and hails from Nambour, the same town in Queensland where Sharlee went to school. He has become a really good bartender and mixologist and this is one of the many punches he came up with after finding out what elderflower was all about. For a big pitcher I'd multiply this recipe by four.

2 lime wedges

45 ml (1½ fl oz) good-quality vodka (I like 666 Pure Tasmanian)

25 ml (¾ fl oz) Elderflower cordial (page 237)

ice cubes

150 ml (5 fl oz) soda water (club soda)

edible flower, to garnish

Squeeze one of the lime wedges into a large wine glass. Pour over the vodka and cordial, fill the glass with ice and top it up with the soda water, then garnish with the remaining lime wedge and a pretty edible flower.

Pictured on page 228

Lizzie's perfect G&T

SERVES 1

> **MR** My gosh, what a G&T this is! I learned it from Lizzie, a good friend of Lizette of schnitzel fame (page 154). A good balloon wine glass is a must to serve this in.

10 ice cubes

finely grated zest of ½ lime

60 ml (2 fl oz) good-quality gin (such as Four Pillars or Melbourne Gin Company)

about 200 ml (7 fl oz) good-quality tonic water

Add the ice cubes and lime zest to a large wine glass and stir together. Leave to sit briefly, then pour over the gin and top up with the tonic, stirring as you go.

Pictured on page 229

My kinda spritz

SERVES 1

> **MR** Less boozy than most alcoholic drinks and so refreshing, I do like a spritz. This one reminds me a little of the '80s growing up – I'm pretty sure it's similar to what my Mum had in her hand – and I like to make it with different base drinks like Lillet Blanc, sherry, dry white wine or even vermouth.

ice cubes

about 125 ml (4 fl oz/ ½ cup) Lilllet Blanc, sherry, vermouth or dry white or red wine

about 125 ml (4 fl oz/ ½ cup) lemonade

1 thick orange slice, to garnish

Fill a large wine glass with the ice cubes and top up with the alcohol and lemonade (you may need a little more or less depending on the size of the glass – just be sure to add them in equal quantities). Garnish with an orange slice and drink.

Pictured on page 228

Dirty martini

SERVES 1

> **MR** I seriously love this drink. Dirty is the way forward.

1 handful ice cubes

60 ml (2 fl oz) good-quality gin (I like those from Four Pillars and the Melbourne Gin Company)

10 ml (¼ fl oz) dry vermouth (I like Maidenii)

10 ml (¼ fl oz) green olive brine, plus extra if necessary

2 green olives, to garnish

Add the ice cubes to a cocktail shaker, pour over the gin and give everything ten solid stirs with a cocktail spoon. Add the vermouth and olive brine and stir again, then taste and add a little more brine if you like your martini dirtier. Strain into a chilled martini glass and garnish with the olives. Drink quickly, then make another.

Pope's kimchi bloody mary

SERVES 1

MR At Pope Joan we leave our tomato juice in the fridge to infuse with all the additions for up to two weeks so that all the flavours get to meld together, but straight up like this is good too. For a virgin mary, just leave out the vodka.

45 ml (1½ fl oz) good-quality vodka (I like 666 Pure Tasmanian)

70 ml (2¼ fl oz) tomato juice

30 ml (1 fl oz) The Fermentary kimchi juice (optional)

juice of ¼ lime, plus a wedge to garnish

5 dashes worcestershire sauce

3–6 dashes Tabasco chilli sauce (depending on how hot you like it)

dash celery bitters (optional)

ice cubes

small pinch of cracked black pepper

small pinch of salt flakes

celery stalk or cucumber stick, to garnish

Add the vodka, tomato juice, kimchi juice, lime juice, worcestershire sauce, Tabasco and celery bitters, if using, to a nice tall glass, fill with ice and stir everything together. Sprinkle over the cracked black pepper and salt flakes and garnish with a lime wedge and a celery stalk or a stick of cucumber.

Raspberry & lemon verbena cordial

MAKES 1 X 750 ML (25½ FL OZ/3 CUPS) BOTTLE

> **MR** We have had a home-made cordial on the menu at Pope Joan since opening in 2010, changing it up with whatever seasonal herbs and fruits we have to hand. This raspberry and lemon verbena number is a highlight of summer for me and makes for a seriously refreshing spritzer when topped up with your choice of water. (While a little gin or vodka added in here truly is the bomb.)

200 g (7 oz) raspberries, fresh or frozen

20 lemon verbena leaves

300 g (10½ oz) caster (superfine) sugar

juice of 2 lemons

TO SERVE (PER PERSON)

3 tablespoons Raspberry and Lemon Verbena Cordial (see above)

ice cubes

400 ml (13½ fl oz) water (regular, sparkling, soda or tonic)

Put everything in a food processor and blitz to a purée. Transfer to a saucepan and bring to the boil, then remove from the heat and leave to cool.

Once cool, sieve the cordial into a measuring cup, then pour it into a sterilised bottle and refrigerate until needed (it will keep for months).

To serve, add 3 tablespoons of the cordial to a tall glass filled with ice cubes and top it up with your choice of water.

Warm hot chocolate

SERVES 2 LITTLE HOOLIGANS

> **MR** This makes a lovely warm (not hot) chocolate and chills well to make a good chocolate milk too. As I get older I never want to stop hearing Finn's and Jay's voices in my head as they are right now asking, 'Can we go to Pope Joan for a hot chocolate that's just warm through, Dad?', in a quiet whisper so that Mum can't hear.

250 ml (8½ fl oz/1 cup) milk

100 ml (3½ fl oz) cream

1½ tablespoons water

2 teaspoons cocoa powder

2 teaspoons sugar

½ teaspoon vanilla paste, (optional)

60 g (2 oz) good-quality dark chocolate, roughly chopped

Bring the milk and cream to a simmer in a saucepan over a medium heat.

Mix the water and cocoa powder together in small bowl to form a paste, then whisk this into the milk mixture together with the remaining ingredients. Stir everything together until the chocolate has melted, then pass through a fine sieve and divide between mugs.

Basics

Elderflower cordial

MAKES ABOUT 1.25 LITRES (42 FL OZ/5 CUPS)

750 g (1 lb 11 oz) sugar

15 g (½ oz) citric acid

25 elderflower heads, tips and flowers only, washed

Put the sugar and citric acid in a pot with 1 litre (34 fl oz/ 4 cups) water. Bring to the boil over a medium heat, stirring to make sure the sugar has dissolved.

Place the elderflower tips and flowers in a heatproof bowl and pour the hot liquid over. Cover and leave to infuse at room temperature until cool.

Pass the liquid through a fine sieve into a clean pot. Bring back to the boil, then pour into sterilised jars and seal.

Keep in a cool dark place for up to 6 months. Once opened, store in the fridge for up to 6 weeks.

Herb salt

MAKES 325 G (11½ OZ)

150 ml (5 fl oz) vegetable oil

160 g (5½ oz) rosemary, sage or oregano, leaves only

90 g (3 oz/ ⅔ cup) salt flakes

Heat the oil in a shallow frying pan over a medium heat and bring to a temperature of 160°C (320°F), or until a cube of bread browns in 45 seconds.

Add the herbs and deep-fry until crispy, about 5–7 minutes, then remove them from the pan with a slotted spoon and place them on a tray lined with paper towels to drain briefly.

Transfer the herbs to a tea towel (dish towel) to dry further, then place in a mortar and pestle with the salt and crush together to combine.

Store in an airtight container and use as you would regular salt. Use within 3 months.

Mr Wilkinson's brown sauce

MAKES ENOUGH TO FILL TWO 325 ML (11 FL OZ) JARS

400 g (14 oz) cooking apples (such as granny smith), cored and roughly chopped

175 g (6 oz) prunes

210 g (7½ oz) white onions, diced

325 ml (11 fl oz) malt vinegar

1 teaspoon ground ginger

½ teaspoon ground allspice

¼ teaspoon cayenne pepper

20 g (¾ oz) salt flakes

220 g (8 oz) tamarind paste

75 g (2¾ oz) molasses

Place the apples, prunes and onions in a heavy-based 3 litre (101 fl oz/12 cup) capacity saucepan over a medium heat. Cover with water and bring to the boil, then reduce the heat and simmer for 25 minutes, or until all the ingredients are soft.

Strain, discarding the liquid, then add the mixture to a food processor or blender and blitz to a fine purée. Return the mixture to the pan with all the other ingredients, bring back to a simmer and cook for 60–80 minutes or until nice and thick, stirring occasionally so as not to burn the base of the pan.

Take off the heat, pour into sterilised jars and seal. Store the brown sauce in the cupboard until needed. Once opened, store in the fridge and use within 3 months.

Mr Wilkinson's kasundi

MAKES ENOUGH TO FILL THREE 325 ML (11 FL OZ) JARS

125 g (4½ oz) fresh ginger, peeled and chopped

70 g (2½ oz) garlic

20 g (¾ oz) green chillies, cut in half and seeded

200 ml (7 fl oz) non-GMO canola oil

1 tablespoon ground turmeric

50 g (1¾ oz/ ½ cup) ground cumin

1 teaspoon chilli powder

1.2 kg (2 lb 10 oz) tinned chopped tomatoes

40 g (1½ oz/ ⅓ cup) salt flakes

300 ml (10 fl oz) apple-cider vinegar

150 g (5½ oz) unrefined soft brown sugar

Chop the ginger, garlic and chilli in a food processor until a smooth paste forms. Set aside.

Warm the canola oil in a heavy-based 3 litre (101 fl oz/12 cup) capacity saucepan over a medium heat. Add the turmeric, cumin and chilli powder and gently toast for 5 minutes to release the natural oils. Stir in the ginger mixture and cook for another 5 minutes.

Add the tomatoes, salt, vinegar and sugar. Bring to the boil, then reduce the heat and simmer for 1–1½ hours. When the oil has risen to the top and the mixture looks like a curry, the pickle is ready.

Take off the heat, pour into sterilised jam jars and seal. The kasundi will keep in a cupboard for at least a year. Once opened, store in the fridge and use within 3 months.

Mr Wilkinson's red sauce
(a.k.a. tomato relish)

MAKES ENOUGH TO FILL TWO 325 ML (11 FL OZ) JARS

500 g (1 lb 2 oz) tomatoes, roughly chopped

1 apple, peeled, cored and roughly chopped

1 white onion, peeled and diced

100 g (3½ oz) raw (demerara) sugar

70 ml (2¼ fl oz) apple-cider vinegar

1 teaspoon salt flakes

pinch of cayenne pepper

pinch of ground black pepper

pinch of ground allspice

pinch of ground cloves

Place everything into a heavy-based 3 litre (101 fl oz/12 cup) capacity saucepan over a medium–low heat. Bring to the boil then reduce to a simmer and cook, stirring occasionally, for 1½ hours until it has a chutney-like consistency.

Take off the heat, pour into sterilised jam jars and seal. The red sauce will keep in a cupboard for at least a year. Once opened, store in the fridge and use within 3 months.

The Mrs' toasted couscous salad

SERVES 4

20 ml (¾ fl oz) olive oil, plus extra for drizzling

185 g (6½ oz/1 cup) instant couscous

250 ml (8½ fl oz/1 cup) boiling water

40 g (1½ oz/ ¼ cup) almonds, roughly chopped

1 tablespoon sunflower seeds, lightly toasted

1 tablespoon sesame seeds, lightly toasted

30 g (1 oz/ ¼ cup) sultanas (golden raisins)

100 g (3½ oz) soft marinated feta, crumbled

juice of ½ lemon

10 chives, finely chopped

1 small handful flat-leaf (Italian) parsley leaves, chopped

Salt flakes and freshly ground black pepper

Heat the oil in a frying pan over a medium heat. Add the couscous and toast for 5 minutes, or until the grains turn a light golden brown. Tip the couscous into a deep large bowl.

Pour over 250 ml (8½ fl oz/1 cup) boiling water, then cover with a plate and let sit for 10 minutes. Remove the plastic and fluff the grains using a fork, until all the grains are separated and there are no clumps.

Add all the remaining ingredients and season with salt flakes and freshly ground black pepper. Mix carefully but thoroughly, then taste – you may need to add an extra splash of olive oil to moisten the couscous a little. Serve.

Smoked tomatoes

MAKES AS MUCH AS YOU NEED

ripe roma (plum) tomatoes, white central cores cut out

caster (superfine) sugar, for sprinkling

salt flakes and freshly ground black pepper

a good handful of woodchips suitable for smoking

To smoke the tomatoes, you'll need a 2 litre (68 fl oz/8 cup) pot, a bowl filled with icy cold water, a roasting tray large enough to hold your tomatoes (but small enough to still fit in your fridge), a wire rack that will fit inside your roasting tin, and a spare shelf in your fridge.

Preheat the oven to 230°C (440°F/Gas 8).

Fill your pot with 1 litre (34 fl oz/4 cups) water and bring to the boil over a high heat. Lower your tomatoes into the water, being careful of hot splashes, and leave for 10 seconds. Scoop out with a slotted spoon and submerge the tomatoes in the iced water to blanch them.

Now peel the tomatoes, then rub each one with sugar, salt flakes and freshly ground black pepper. Place them on the wire rack.

Heat the smoking chips in a wok or frying pan. When they start to smoke, tip them into your roasting tray, then sit the rack of tomatoes on top. Cover with foil, pierce five holes in the foil, then it's into the oven for 5 minutes. Take out straight away.

Place the roasting tray in the fridge, on a thick tea towel (dish towel) so your fridge shelves don't melt. Leave until the tomatoes are cool. So now you have smoked tomatoes! They will keep in an airtight container in the fridge for about 7 days.

XO sauce

MAKES 500 ML (17 FL OZ/2 CUPS)

250 g (9 oz) mushrooms (shiitake, wild pine or Swiss browns), diced

4 teaspoons salt flakes

300 ml (10 fl oz) vegetable oil

50 g (1¾ oz) fresh ginger, peeled and cut into thin strips

8 garlic cloves, crushed

3 teaspoons chilli flakes

50 g (1¾ oz) dried black beans, soaked in water for 24 hours then rinsed

60 ml (2 fl oz/ ¼ cup) fish sauce

3 tablespoons soy sauce

1 tablespoon raw (demerara) sugar

60 ml (2 fl oz/ ¼ cup) rice vinegar

Place the mushrooms in a colander, add the salt, stir thoroughly and let sit for 3 hours. Now wash under cold water and let dry.

Heat half the oil in a saucepan over a low heat, add the ginger and cook for 5–7 minutes until golden and caramelised. Add the garlic and chilli, lower the heat and cook for 5 minutes more, stirring frequently, then return the heat to medium, add the mushrooms and cook until they start to break down, about 7 minutes.

Add the beans and cook for a further 5 minutes, then add the fish sauce, soy, sugar and rice vinegar. Bring to the boil, reduce the heat to a low simmer and cook for 12 minutes until everything is nicely combined. Remove from the heat and leave to cool, then stir in the remaining oil. Transfer to a sterilised jar or container and place in the fridge until needed (it will keep for ages and I reckon it tastes better the longer you leave it).

Baked beans

SERVES 4

150 ml (5 fl oz) olive oil

1 white onion, sliced

½ teaspoon smoked paprika

½ teaspoon ground black pepper

½ teaspoon ground allspice

¼ teaspoon ground cumin

¼ teaspoon ground turmeric

½ teaspoon salt flakes

1 tablespoon tomato paste (concentrated purée)

50 g raw (demerara) sugar

115 ml (4 fl oz) red wine vinegar

400 g (14 oz) tinned crushed tomatoes

400 g (14 oz) tinned cannellini (lima) or butter beans, drained

Heat the oil in a saucepan over a medium heat, add the onion and sauté for 5 minutes or until soft. Add the spices and salt and cook, stirring, for 3–4 minutes, then add the tomato paste and cook for a further 2 minutes. Add the sugar and vinegar, increase the heat and cook until the liquid has been reduced to a glaze, then add the tinned tomatoes and 200 ml (7 fl oz) water and bring to the boil. Cook for 8–12 minutes until the sauce has a nice, thick consistency, then add the tinned beans and warm through. Leave to sit for 5 minutes before serving.

Mayo

MAKES ABOUT 420 G (15 OZ)

2 free-range egg yolks

2 teaspoons dijon mustard

375 ml (12½ fl oz/1½ cups) sunflower oil or mild-flavoured vegetable oil

20 ml (¾ fl oz) good-quality white wine vinegar

In a bowl, whisk together the egg yolks and mustard until the yolks turn pale. Slowly whisk in the oil until fully combined, then add the vinegar and season to your liking – I prefer to just add sea salt. The mayo will keep for 1 week in an airtight jar in the fridge.

Harissa

MAKES 250 ML (8½ FL OZ/1 CUP)

50 g (1¾ oz) jarred chilli paste

6 preserved red capsicums (bell peppers)

½ teaspoon tomato paste (concentrated purée)

½ teaspoon cumin seeds

1 teaspoon salt

1 teaspoon sugar

2 garlic cloves

2 tablespoons white-wine vinegar

75 ml (2½ fl oz/ ⅓ cup) extra-virgin olive oil

Add all the ingredients except the olive oil to a blender and whiz together to form a paste. Stir through the olive oil to finish. Store in the fridge in a sealed container for up to 6 months.

Guacamole

SERVES 4

1 avocado

juice of ½ lime

1 tablespoon natural yoghurt

pinch of salt flakes

Cut the avocado in half, remove the stone and scoop the flesh into a bowl, then add the lime, yoghurt and salt and mash together with a fork.

Polenta

SERVES 4

150 g (5½ oz/1 cup) instant polenta

1 tablespoon extra-virgin olive oil

50 g (1¾ oz) freshly grated parmesan cheese, plus extra to serve

1 teaspoon salt flakes

Bring 1.25 litres (42 fl oz/5 cups) water to boil in a very large saucepan. Whisking constantly, pour in the polenta and, when it starts to bubble, reduce the heat and continue to cook for 15 minutes, whisking as you go, until thick and smooth. Add the olive oil, parmesan and salt and whisk hard for 30 seconds to combine.

Proper mash

SERVES 4

600 g (1 lb 5 oz) all-purpose potatoes, peeled and cut into 3 cm (1¼ in) dice

115 g (4 oz) salted butter, finely diced

80 ml (2½ fl oz/ ⅓ cup) milk

large pinch of salt flakes

For the mash, place the potatoes in a saucepan and wash in cold water to get rid of any excess starch. Drain, then cover the potatoes with water by 5 cm (2 in). Bring the potatoes to a boil over a high heat, then reduce to a simmer and cook for 15 minutes, or until the potatoes are soft. Remove from the heat and drain, then return the potatoes to the pan and leave on the stove top to dry out. Using a potato ricer or masher, mash the potatoes until smooth then whisk in the butter, milk and salt.

A NOTE ON PROPER MASH FROM MATT ...
There's mash, then there's mash. Chefs make really good mash. First up, you need a starchy-style potato as they make a fluffier, smoother mash. Try a Dutch cream, an otway red, a king edward or a yukon gold – when these are in season, they are no-fail mashing potatoes for me. Another key is to remove all excess water by boiling and straining your potatoes then placing them back on the stove and warming them over a low heat to steam (this makes the mash less watery in flavour and texture). Then there is the butter ... add lots, you want the butter starting to separate from the mash before bringing it back with a little milk or cream (every now and then I add a wedge of spreadable cheese like Happy Cow in here too). Lastly is the amount of salt. A good chef's pinch of salt (see page 216 for details) with mash and please, no pepper.

ACKNOWLEDGEMENTS

Much love and thanks to our publishing team at Hardie Grant – Jane, Mark, Andrea and Simon for pursuing this project with us and making it awesome.

Thank you to our design team, Paul and Rachel from Racket, for their creativity and brilliance. They had a great sense of our home and family life, and captured it on the page.

For the book shoot we had the A-team. Thanks to the best stylist in the biz, Caroline Velik, we were in prop heaven, and ace photographer Patricia (Patsy) Niven lit up the room and captured how it really is at home. Thanks to her trusty assistant and wordsmith, Rich MacDonald.

Thanks also to Nonna Leah, who was on hooligan duty during the shoot and our school Mum gang for their support, play dates and for consuming leftovers.

Special mentions to all the fab people who shared a recipe with us for the book: Jase, Jo, Lizette, Lizzie, Jimmy, Deano, Avi, Carol, Leah and Edna.

A big thank you to the amazing team at Pope Joan, especially Jase, Jake and Morgan, for their hard work and endless commitment to making a difference in the way people eat and think about eating. We love you guys. And yes, Marek Holba for making a joke about his name in my last book, love you bud.

And lastly, so many hugs and kisses to our favourite people in the world: our rocks; our critics; our cheer squads; our extended family; our friends. You know who you are, but special hugs over this time must go to Nessie, Fran, Matt and Lentil, Dan and Bez, Fab, Travis, the Snaithys and old man Steve.

ABOUT THE AUTHORS

MATT WILKINSON

Originally hailing from Yorkshire in northern England, Matt Wilkinson is a chef, author and passionate advocate for ethical farming. He loves nothing more than getting his hands dirty gardening, camping and fishing and has never been one to say no to a martini. Matt is the owner of Pope Joan and The Pie Shop in Melbourne's East Brunswick, the author of *Mr Wilkinson's Favourite Vegetables* and *Mr Wilkinson's Simply Dressed Salads,* and a contributing writer for *Delicious* magazine. This is his third cookbook.

SHARLEE GIBB

Sharlee Gibb grew up on Queensland's Sunshine Coast. At 18, she stumbled into the world of food and travelled the world working in hospitality. A keen cook, Sharlee trained under Darina Allen at her famed Ballymaloe Cookery School in Ireland before forging a career off the pans as an event manager and curator. A former Gastronomy Program Manager for the Melbourne Food & Wine Festival, Sharlee now runs her own events business curateEAT, is a regular contributor to Eater and Luckie and she is the founder of Fully Booked Women – a community for women in the food and drink industry. This is her first cookbook.

INDEX

NOTES

Published in 2017 by Hardie Grant Books, an imprint of Hardie Grant Publishing

Hardie Grant Books (Melbourne)
Building 1, 658 Church Street
Richmond, Victoria 3121
hardiegrantbooks.com

Hardie Grant Books (London)
5th & 6th Floors
52–54 Southwark Street
London SE1 1UN
hardiegrantbooks.com

A Cataloguing-in-Publication entry is available from the catalogue of the National Library of Australia at www.nla.gov.au

Mr & Mrs Wilkinson's How it is at Home
ISBN 978 1 74379 289 6

Publishing Director: Jane Willson
Managing Editor: Marg Bowman
Project Editor: Andrea O'Connor
Editor: Simon Davis
Design Manager: Mark Campbell
Designers: Racket
Illustrations: Paul Mosig
Photographer: Patricia Niven
Production Manager: Todd Rechner
Production Coordinator: Rebecca Bryson

Colour reproduction by Splitting Image Colour Studio
Printed in China by 1010 Printing International Limited